Carl Bereiter co-authored, with Siegfried Englemann, *Teaching Disadvantaged Children in the Preschool* (Prentice-Hall, 1966), was the principal author of a book on kindergarten educational programs, and is the author of over 50 published articles on early childhood education, educational policy, and educational research. He has held a Guggenheim Fellowship, 1968, and a fellowship at the Center for Advanced Study in the Behavioral Sciences, 1973–74, and was on the staff of the Ontario Institute for Studies in Education.

MUST WE EDUCATE?

Carl Bereiter

Prentice-Hall, Inc. A SPECTRUM BOOK *Englewood Cliffs, N.J.*

Library of Congress Cataloging in Publication Data

BEREITER, CARL.
Must we educate?

(A Spectrum Book)
Includes bibliographical references.
1. Education, Elementary—United States.
2. Elementary school teaching. I. Title.
LA219.B47 1973 372.9'73 73–14824
ISBN 0–13–608372–2
ISBN 0–13–608364–1 (pbk.)

10 9 8 7 6 5 4 3 2 1

PRENTICE-HALL INTERNATIONAL, INC. (*London*)
PRENTICE-HALL OF AUSTRALIA, PTY. LTD. (*Sydney*)
PRENTICE-HALL OF CANADA, LTD. (*Toronto*)
PRENTICE-HALL OF INDIA PRIVATE LIMITED (*New Delhi*)
PRENTICE-HALL OF JAPAN, INC. (*Tokyo*)

PREFACE

For those who know of my earlier work on teaching disadvantaged children, some explanation is needed to relate what I am saying now to what I was saying seven years ago. The program of the academic preschool that Siegfried Engelmann and I ran has been labeled a "pressure-cooker" and a "Marine drill-sergeant" approach to teaching. Those are exaggerated characterizations of a school that aimed at giving children lively, direct training in basic academic skills. It is fair, however, to say that our approach represented the very antithesis of the informal child-centered approach so dear to educational liberals and radicals.

I still think that if you want to teach a skill the direct approach is the best way to do it. That is how most training is carried out in the real world—in swimming classes, music lessons, and on-the-job training—where training works. The indirect approach currently favored by schools simply cheats kids by putting too great a burden on their own initiative and ability to figure things out.

What I have never felt good about is making kids over in the interests of an educational program. Undiscriminating readers like Edgar Z. Friedenberg and William Labov saw our approach as imposing middle-class standards on lower-class kids. In fact, our approach does just the opposite—and that is both its strength and its weakness. It leaves kids alone. It doesn't try to alter their language or behavior in any general way but tries merely to teach skills and behaviors that will be useful to them as students.

Lower-class black kids remain lower-class black kids, only they become literate. We don't try to condition them in the process to some ideal of middle-class childhood or to some romanticized form of black culture. Although there may be some value in it I don't see such conditioning as our prerogative or the prerogative of any public school system. The weakness of this hands-off approach is that children don't change in fundamental ways. If direct training ceases and children are left in the sink-or-swim environment of the modern classroom, they tend to sink as other children like them do. They haven't been made over into the kinds of children who fare well in such an environment.

What can be done? The options are fairly clear and whether we make kids over, continue direct training, or give up and say, "Who needs to read anyway?" the choice is a moral one, not a technical one. This book is essentially a study of this moral dilemma, one that applies to all children and not only to the most needy. I see "making kids over" as another label for "educating the whole child." I'm opposed to it because it is incompatible with the values of a free society to force on all children the prevailing notions of how people should be. Are there any humane and practical alternatives—alternatives that respect the right of people to be themselves yet at the same time meet societal needs and give people a chance to realize their own goals? The second part of this book deals with such alternatives—with what amount to alternatives to education.

I have been stressing the continuity between the ideas presented in this book and the ideas underlying my earlier work. In fact, however, my ideas have undergone a long and sometimes wayward evolution. I first began thinking about the fundamental issues during a year of study in 1968 made possible by a Guggenheim Fellowship and a study leave from the Ontario Institute for Studies in Education. My goal at the time was to produce a catalog of objectives for early education. The catalog was never produced, for in working toward it I began reading John Dewey and thus, inevitably, began to question the whole notion of ultimate goals. The ideas set forth in the present book began to form when I undertook a critique of the Hall-Dennis report, a document that set forth for the Ontario school system the goals of child-centered education. An eloquent, humane document, the report nevertheless struck me as a dangerous one that would impose a liberal upper middle-class ideology on the diverse cultures of Ontario.

The next major influence on my thinking came from contact with Ivan Illich and Everett Reimer. In visits to Cuernavaca in 1970 and 1971 I came to appreciate the power of the idea of "unpackaging" educational services, and to think for the first time about the dubious role of service institutions in modern societies. The influence of these ideas will be evident through this book. The book took its final form in a seminar I conducted at the Harvard Summer School in 1972 on "Reform of Educational Objectives."

Many people have stimulated my thinking, but I am mainly aware of the critical impact of Philip Jackson, Lawrence Kohlberg, and Robert Kegan. These are people with differing but powerful and well-grounded beliefs in education—beliefs that I have found impossible to reject and to which I have, therefore, had to accommodate my own beliefs, in ways that I am sure are unsatisfactory to them. I also owe much to Helen Bereiter for her continuing interest and support and for making possible the kind of life that made this book possible. Finally, I owe an inestimable debt to Ann Hughes, who in her life sustained me with her eager mind and her love of life, and who in her death left me with the desire to do something worthy of her faith in me.

Toronto
April, 1973

TABLE OF CONTENTS

[E]ducation is unmatched in the extent to which it molds the personality of the youth of society. While police and fire protection, garbage collection and street lights are essentially neutral in their effect on the individual psyche, public education actively attempts to shape a child's personal development in a manner chosen not by the child or his parents but by the state.

California Supreme Court
Serrano v. Priest

PART I

THE MORAL DILEMMA IN EDUCATION

chapter one

Must We Educate?

Each of us has an interest in the kinds of adults our neighbors' children will become. If they turn out to be criminals or incompetents we pay for it. If they turn out to be responsible citizens we benefit—or our children benefit, which comes to the same thing. But, although we have this interest, as individuals we have no right to act upon it. We do not have the right to take our neighbors' children in hand and shape them into the kinds of adults that we happen to prefer.

Most people would agree, I think, that that is how it should be for neither would we like our neighbor, with his crotchety or benighted ideas, to be able to work his will on our own children. But if our neighbor happens to be a school teacher, not only does he have the right to try to shape our children, it is his universally acknowledged and widely applauded job to do so. Yet our teacher-neighbor is a human being not much different from our other neighbors, with the same weaknesses and biases and, perhaps, with the same misgivings deep inside about taking the destinies of other people's children into his own hands.

This is a peculiar business. It can be reasoned that we have delegated our parental authority to the teacher. However, we didn't personally do so; rather, we are required by law to do so. But, you may argue, almost everybody concurs with this legal requirement because it is the only practical way to educate children. This argument has merit, but the word educate is tricky. It includes more than we bargain for. We want our children to be taken care of during the day and we want them to learn. But let us consider the other people to whom we assign duties similar to a teacher's. For instance, there may be another neighbor who gives piano lessons and a neighbor's daughter who baby-sits our children on occasion. These people take care of our children and teach them certain things, but we have not delegated to them any general authority to determine the kinds of adults our children ought to become. If they start trying to shape our children's development in any general way, we feel they are stepping out of bounds just as much as if our neighbor the plumber tried to do such a thing. How, then, has the school teacher come to acquire such a special power?

An answer to this question will be provided for us if we try to keep our children out of school. We will, of course, be taken into court for breaking the law. If we try to argue that we have decided we can do without the services of the school, that our children seem to be able to learn what they need to with only a little help from us, and that we do not mind having them around the house all day, we will be told that education is not a public service, but a state prerogative. We will be told that high courts have affirmed that the state has a duty and right to educate children to ensure that they become competent, responsible citizens.

It begins to appear that our interest in the upbringing of our neighbors' children does indeed have some force behind it, although this force is not exercised individually but collectively through the state. If we begin to investigate how this force is exercised in our behalf, we will discover something else that is quite strange. We will find all kinds of authorities who have been elected or appointed to determine how our children are to be educated. They shuffle papers and hold meetings with one another, but they do not have the faintest knowledge of what our neighbor-teacher is doing with our children in the classroom. At the level of the local school itself, we find a principal who has ideas about how children should be educated, but they are his own ideas not our ideas and not the ideas of some collectivity that represents us. Furthermore, he may not have very much idea what is going on in the classroom either because it is going on behind a closed door. It turns out in practice that the "state" which is supposed to be educating our children is none other than the teacher himself.

Thus certain people, little different from ourselves, have been given a power denied to the rest of us to shape the development of other people's children. This special status is connected, obviously, with the fact that they teach and take care of children. But, as we have seen, there are other people who teach children or take care of them who do not have any special right to influence their general development. That is to say, they are entitled by our consent to train or to watch over our children, but not to *educate* them.

In this book I do not propose to inquire into how school teachers came to acquire the right to educate children. This is not a history. What I propose to do is to question that right, to look at its implications, and to consider alternatives. However, this book is not a criticism of schools as such. Schools are but a mechanism of public education; even if they were replaced by other mechanisms the basic issues would remain. It is public education itself that I want to question.

The schools have been subjected to a great deal of criticism recently, and for a while, the criticism was so intense that it began to look as if the schools might fold up under it. It is now apparent, however, that nothing of the sort is going to happen in the near future. Liberal reforms are making the schools more liveable and, thus, taking away much of the pressure for radical change. Even if the poor are not getting anything more out of school than they did before, they are not getting noticeably less, and so their dissatisfaction with the schools is not producing any greater strains. The sense of emergency seems to be passing; there is time now to reflect and to think more deeply about the place of education in modern societies. This book is not a call to arms, but a call to the armchair. It is time, I think, to pause from asking how society can educate its children better and to consider whether society must educate its children at all.

What Is Education?

Already in this introduction I have used familiar words in a way that runs against common understanding. I have spoken of people being entitled "to train or to watch over children, but not to *educate* them." Aren't training and child care part of education? How can you separate them? Well, to be sure, you can't arrange a school schedule to have training and child care in the morning and education in the afternoon. Education is doing something, and training and child care are two of the things that people often do in the process of education.

Education is a matter of purpose and focus. To educate a child is to act with the purpose of influencing the child's development as a whole person. What you do may vary. You may teach him, you may play with him, you may structure his environment, you may censor his television viewing, or you may pass laws to keep him out of bars. But you may do any of these things for purposes other than to educate the child. That is why you cannot just peek in on someone and tell whether or not he is engaged in education. You have to watch him for some time and perhaps even question him to see what he is up to.

When we say that the piano teacher and the baby-sitter are not engaged in education, we mean that they are not out to influence in any profound way the kind of person that the child is becoming. The piano teacher is trying to inculcate a certain skill. How that skill is to be integrated into the child's life or what effect it may have on his overall personal development are matters over which the piano teacher does not normally try to exert any influence. To the extent that he does, he is stepping beyond his role as trainer and is trying to educate. The baby-sitter is concerned with the child's behavior and experience in the here-and-now. This does not mean that she tends the child as if he were a goat. If she is a good baby-sitter she makes the child's time with her rewarding and meaningful; but the rewards and the meaning are all in the present experience and not in some future state of development toward which she is bending the child.

A parent may have ideas about how he wants his child to develop, and may choose the piano teacher and the baby-sitter with great care in order to advance the child's development along the desired lines. In that case, the parent is engaged in education and choosing the piano teacher and the baby-sitter are educational acts. But the piano teacher and the baby-sitter are not acting as educators; they are merely instruments that the parent is using in his educational efforts. The child's school teacher, however, is not an instrument used by the parents. Often, in fact, when he sends notes home to the parents asking them to encourage their child to try harder or asking them to drill the child on his times tables, he is in effect asking the parents to serve as instruments to achieve his own educational goals for the children.

Thus, the school teacher has a role that is much superior to that of trainer or child tender. It is a role that does not merely supplement the role of the parents but competes with it and even, perhaps, usurps it. It is the role of "molder of citizens," and "shaper of the next generation"—a role that has been glorified in all the inspirational literature of education and taken for granted in educational philosophy and policy-making. But is it a necessary role and is it a morally acceptable one?

The Moral Dilemma in Education: An Overview

The remainder of this chapter is devoted to an overview of the book. The first part considers moral issues concerning the role of education in a democratic society. The second part considers alternatives to education in the rearing of children and youths. In the overview I do not merely summarize the chapters, but try to show a continuous line of thought that tends to get lost as topics are treated one at a time.

THE SEARCH FOR MORALLY ACCEPTABLE EDUCATIONAL GOALS

The role of the teacher as I have defined it is a very authoritarian one, conjuring up the image of a godlike shaper of destinies. This image does not fit very well the teachers one encounters in real life, Poor View who are apt to display considerable modesty in approaching their tasks. A criticism of education would not have much point if it amounted to nothing more than an indictment of the rare tyrant. Modest though they may be, however, teachers do not present themselves as mere trainers in the "three R's" and caretakers of children. In my experience they claim universally to be concerned with the whole child—with the development of his personality, values, intellect, and future role as an adult.

Wherein, then, lies their modesty? Partly, and realistically, it lies in their recognition that they really cannot do much to influence these major outcomes of development. But that is small comfort, for the day is soon likely to arrive when teachers will have at their disposal far more effective ways of influencing development. Behavior-modification techniques and the techniques of sensitivity training and group encounter point in that direction.

Modesty comes also from another source. Many educators do not believe that they are personally deciding how children should develop and then imposing their decisions on other people's children. Some of them believe that "society" makes these decisions democratically and they merely carry them out. That, of course, is a delusion. More sophisticated educators, however, often claim that they are helping each child develop according to his own nature—or, rather than imposing a single view of his future on the child, that they are helping to increase the possibilities open to him, or to increase his ability to make up his own mind and shape his own future.

These and other apparently laudable educational goals are examined in chapter 2. There I conclude that the only kind of teaching that is truly nonauthoritarian is skill training, for competence in general gives the individual more power and freedom of choice. Even then it appears that in a democratic system the choice of skills should be left up to the learner and not made for him. A person's knowledge, beliefs, values, habits, and personal traits are also significant determinants of his freedom, but they can work for it or against it: they can be confining as well as liberating. Education, therefore, in so far as it deals with these characteristics of a person, should be provided only in the form of options for people who are old enough to choose how they want to change themselves. Thus it would appear that education should not be offered as a public service to children but only for adolescents and adults. Mass education of children is unavoidably authoritarian—a shaping of people according to the aims of those in power.

THE RIGHT TO MAKE MISTAKES

Someone must educate children. It is sheer romance to imagine that they can grow into adequate adults without some guiding influence. Traditionally this guidance comes from the home, and even with universal compulsory schooling the home still appears to be the main educational influence on children. That is how it should be in a free society. A society that granted individuals the right to live according to their own values but did not grant them the right to raise their children according to those values would not be a free society—it would only be a society in which individual liberty was strangled slowly instead of abruptly.

How, then, does it happen in democratic societies that the state has assumed the right to educate children? There are fairly obvious reasons why the state should have an interest in how children turn out, but it does not immediately follow that the state has a right to do anything about it beyond providing cultural resources and, perhaps, financial assistance to parents in educating their children. The answer seems to reside in a widespread conviction, shared by government officials and professional "helpers" of all kinds, that people must not be allowed to make mistakes. The need to keep people from making mistakes has been used for centuries to justify keeping them—slaves, women, whole nations—in bondage. The argument has always proved to have some truth in it. When set free, people have made mistakes; no doubt parents and children set free to make their own educational decisions would make mistakes as well. But increasingly it is recognized that people have a right to freedom nevertheless. It would seem that eventually it must be recognized that the right of people to make mistakes in educating themselves and their children is one that cannot legitimately be withheld.

Even if the majority are satisfied to have educational choices made for them, it does not follow that the state should do so. Educational freedom and religious freedom are parallel cases in this regard. State schools and state churches both inevitably undermine freedom, even if they satisfy a large majority of the people. It seems clear from the standpoint of human rights that public education is an anachronism. Established at a time when individual liberties were not so clearly recognized and not so jealously defended, public education is grossly out of keeping with modern conceptions of freedom.

The most difficult issue of rights is not the issue of parents versus the state but the issue of parents versus their children. The issue is difficult because the child cannot exercise rights from birth but must somehow, at some time in his development, accede to rights that were previously held by his parents. There is no neat solution to the problem of transfer of rights. What I suggest is that children should not necessarily acquire all rights of citizenship at the same time, and that they should acquire educational rights at an earlier age than some other rights. Children begin to take a conscious interest in their own development around the age of thirteen or fourteen and so it would be reasonable for them to have the right to begin making their own educational decisions at about that time. Parents would still have influence, of course, but they would not have authority supported by law. This is a hard nut to swallow because most parents, too, are infected with an unwillingness to let people—particularly their own children—make mistakes. But I don't see any other way to give full meaning to the right of people to determine their own course of development—a right without which most other rights become meaningless.

IS INEQUALITY HERE TO STAY?

The strongest argument against leaving educational decisions in the hands of parents and children is that poorly educated parents will have poorly educated children. Thus, the argument runs, the price of educational freedom will be that the poor will get poorer as the rich get richer.

It is difficult to write this argument off by saying that freedom always has its price. If the costs fall mainly on the poor, that is not a good thing. The poor come off badly even now under a system of universal compulsory education, but it is possible that they could come off still worse. If, however, we look dispassionately at why the poor come off badly under the present system, the evidence is clear that they are deficient in a variety of intellectual and motivational characteristics that constitute scholastic aptitude (of which IQ is only one component).

To remedy all of these deficiencies would be to make poor people over into quite different kinds of people. While they might then be better equipped to succeed in school, whole subcultures would have been destroyed in the process. That is an intolerably high price to pay for something which in the end would make at best a modest contribution to social equality. Recent studies, such as those of Ivar Berg and Christopher Jencks, indicate that education has been greatly overrated as a basis for social success. Our concern with educational equality has produced no tangible gains and has served only to deflect us from more positive social actions in the interests of equality.

A more reasonable goal in the area of education would be to make it possible for all children, regardless of background and regardless of scholastic aptitude, to acquire adequate levels of skill in reading, writing, and practical arithmetic. The means to do this are available, or are becoming available, through careful training. There is no reason to suppose that poor people would not take advantage of training opportunities if these were available to them. Such training would not achieve social equality. However, it could do more than any mild educational treatment and, perhaps, would do as much as can be done in *any* way that respected the right of people to be different.

People have a right to make themselves over, of course, and perhaps the children of poor parents have a right to have their children made over into middle-class types. This would require a very potent kind of education of which a few examples now exist, for instance, in programs where poor children are taken out of their environments and put into expensive private residential schools. But this form of education ought certainly to be only one of several options and not something that is imposed, even in the most watered-down form, on all poor children.

THE INSTITUTIONALIZATION OF PERSONAL CHOICE

How is one to draw the line between public services and public imposition of goals on individuals? The two cannot be entirely separated because in providing any public service decisions have to be made that may influence the development and destinies of people. There are some principles, however, that can be applied to minimize the extent to which public institutions take over the lives of people. One principle, stressed by Ivan Illich, is that institutions should not generate needs for their own services and for other services, thus leading to an ever-increasing dependence on institutions. Illich has proposed radical redesign of institutions, including educational ones, so that they will leave people alone, as public utilities do, instead of absorbing them, as the welfare system does.

I suggest that the key point is to limit the means by which institutions are able to create needs for their services. Schools make people dependent on schooling through monopoly, compulsory attendance, and by issuing credentials that have become requirements of employment. Other institutions create needs by attaching strings to benefits, as the welfare system does, and by advertising, as private industry does. These methods of generating needs are all, in their various ways, disreputable. They could, in all justice, be limited by laws which would leave the way open for services to be offered to the public but that would require them to stand on their merits. This would reduce the threat to individual responsibility and freedom.

Still, in the choice of public services, public officials would find themselves acting as educators. In making a choice between one alternative and another they would be bound to take account of the effect each alternative would have on the development of people, and this would be, by my definition, an educational decision. In this matter we have no choice but to depend on the good faith of people in office. And so the important question becomes, what constitutes good faith? At present we are so committed to a belief in public education that a parks commissioner or a welfare director is considered to be operating in the best of faith if he uses his office to advance generally acceptable notions of how people should be. If we looked at it differently, however, and saw public education as a dangerous intrusion into the lives of individuals, the public officials who acted in such a way would be condemned as readily as those who used their offices for graft. The responsible official would be one who regarded his power to educate in the same way as he regarded his power to make people rich—as a power not to be abused, but to be exercised with as much fairness, impartiality, and restraint as possible.

Alternatives to Education

Perhaps the greatest obstacle to fundamental criticism of education is that there are no immediately obvious alternatives except doing nothing. It is hard to imagine a child doing anything worthwhile that is not educational, and hard to imagine an adult relating to a child in any worthwhile way except to educate him. The second part of this book is devoted to concrete suggestions for things that can be done for children and adolescents apart from educating them. I hope it will be viewed in its proper perspective; that is, as a demonstration that alternatives do exist, and not as the presentation of a program which, if found wanting, can be picked apart and used as a sufficient reason to ignore the issues raised in the first part of the book. There are always alternatives to alternatives, and if the issues are valid they are worth considering in their own right.

SCHOOLS WITHOUT EDUCATION

Children need to be taken care of when they are away from their parents and they need training in some basic skills, mainly the three R's. Elementary schools exist primarily to serve these two needs, but have subordinated them to an overall objective of educating, for which there is no clearly established need. Training in the schools has been poor. Substantial numbers of children have failed to learn the rudimentary skills to an adequate level. The quality of child care has varied. In the days of the birch rod it was abominable. In the past century it has improved, but the schoolhouse rituals on which it is still based are becoming too evidently absurd to survive. Informal education shows promise of being a superior form of child care, although it does not appear to be any improvement as far as training is concerned.

I suggest that both training and child care can be done better if they are handled separately—by different people and according to different styles. By "unpackaging" the two, moreover, education as the all-embracing function of schools becomes lost. I do not think it will be missed. The alternative system would find the typical child involved for a couple of hours a day in lively sessions of training in basic skills, carried out by people who saw themselves not as educators but as capable imparters of competence. The rest of the time the child would be in the care of people similar to camp counselors who would help him take advantage of opportunities for activities inside and outside of school that were worthwhile in their own right rather than aimed at some supposed educational effect.

A BETTER LIFE FOR CHILDREN

What are activities for children that are worthwhile in their own right? They are not merely activities that are fun. I suggest as a criterion that child care should be concerned with increasing the quality of children's immediate experience. By whose standard? Inevitably, by the standard of the people who have control. These will be mainly adults, although children can enter into the process of proposing and judging alternatives.

Thus, what I am proposing is not a neutral or value-free treatment of children. This would be impossible in any event. I am proposing that the cultural life of children should be treated like the cultural life of adults—as something that should have quality, meaning, and moral value in the here-and-now rather than in some future state of development. Cultural facilities and activities should be designed to enable children to make fuller use of the human qualities they already have rather than to develop new qualities. It might be argued that this is simply education under a different guise, but I think the intention is fundamentally different.

Some specific suggestions are made: to provide intellectual recreation in place of schooling, to make it easier for children to do things rather than merely to watch, to provide quiet places without prescribed activities, to encourage age intermixing, and to provide resources that can be used in a variety of unprogrammed as well as programmed ways. There is room for a great deal of creative thinking in planning cultural resources for children once it is recognized that the talents of the educator are not the main talents to be employed.

OPTIONAL ADOLESCENCE

As children grow into adolescence their needs diverge. Some are ready to move directly into adult jobs and marriage. Others need an extended period of career training but want little else in the way of education. Then there are others—the most conspicuous, but actually a minority—who value a lengthy period of freedom from work in order to pursue their own development and to do any of a variety of nonvocational things. If we define adolescence as this in between period of freedom from vocational responsibility it is obvious that some want it and others do not.

At the present time the choice is not a free one. If you want to be an adolescent you have to be a student, and vice-versa. Consequently our high schools and colleges are glutted with young people who don't particularly want schooling but who want the kind of adolescent life and the kinds of future careers that schooling makes possible. The U.S. Supreme Court has already judged that competence, not schooling, should be the criterion for employment. If this judgment is applied fully, it would relieve one of the binds that young people are in. But to make adolescence truly optional it should also be possible for young people to enjoy their freedom without having to go to school. I suggest unrestricted grants for this purpose, to be repaid through a surtax on income in later years.

Other options to meet other needs are university-type schooling for the minority seriously interested in studying academic disciplines, a service corps to provide socially meaningful work, and opportunities for vocational training and on-the-job training. This set of options may raise fears of the emergence of a caste system, but I think such fears are realistic only under a system where academic education is the sole route to social status. When that is not the case, optional adolescence would make it possible for more people with nonacademic inclinations to experience the period of adolescent development that so sharply separates the social classes in contemporary society.

To permit young people to be adolescents without going to school would be to turn them loose on a world that is afraid of them. But it appears that the world is going to have to come to terms with adolescents as a subcultural group anyway. Society could stand to benefit from what adolescents have to offer instead of fighting a losing battle to keep them in check.

EDUCATION AND SOCIETY'S NEEDS

What education does for the individual is one thing; what it does for society is another. We look to education to solve social problems by changing people. It does not work very well and, in general, problems of human behavior are better dealt with by changing the incentives according to which people act. There are times when a whole population might need to be changed—for instance, to make people less inclined toward violence. Such changes, however, would require a great deal more than schooling. They would require overhauling virtually every aspect of societal functioning. It is unlikely that a free society would ever take such a change upon itself. To support public education as a partial measure is simply to feed an expensive illusion.

We also look to education to provide a productive work force. What has happened, however, is that educational processing has taken the place of competence. If the emphasis were shifted back to demonstrated ability, with opportunities available for training and testing, the likely result would be a general increase in competence.

Societies are coming to depend more and more on the growth of knowledge to meet their needs. The growth of knowledge should not be confused with education, however. The two can go on quite separately. It merely happens that an important part of the growth of knowledge, university research, is supported by funds ostensibly intended for education. This fact needs to be taken into account, however, when considering alternatives that would drastically reduce the amount of money going into higher education. Society would have to start paying for its knowledge directly, which it has never proved willing to do in the past. The dependence of research upon educational funds makes an awkward situation. I do not know of a good solution, but it does not seem reasonable to propose that the public should go on indefinitely paying for something it does not really need in order to obtain as a side benefit something that it does need.

Finally, education has often been looked to as a means of keeping the classical heritage alive. What is at issue here is not only preservation of the old but infusion of the present with wisdom and with ideas of greatness. To many people, giving up on the effort to educate means consigning modern society to mediocrity, materialism, and short-sightedness. I sense this danger very strongly, but it seems to me that mass education has not been and cannot possibly be the answer. Its effect is to dilute the classical tradition to the point where it is ineffectual. I would rather put my faith in serious humanistic study for the few who want it and, for society as a whole, trust that high ideals will ultimately prove more attractive than low. That is a slim hope, but I do not see that we have any other.

WILL ANYTHING HAPPEN?

What will happen to education is anybody's guess, but there are definite trends suggesting eventual decline of public education. Rising costs, together with declining public concern for education as knowledge becomes a less scarce commodity, may lead to paring down schooling to training in basic skills. High schools may become more like colleges and other options may have to be established as more rapidly maturing adolescents insist on their rights. If the trend toward more experimentation in life styles continues, we will have a new kind of cultural pluralism that will make mass education less acceptable. Many of the new life styles stress values of life in the here-and-now—values that run counter to educational values. Finally, as we develop more powerful techniques for changing people, education is likely to be seen as an outright danger rather than as the merely benign or vaguely unobjectionable thing it is now. Although these trends suggest changes in the directions I have proposed, all outcomes are in doubt. Therefore it is worth giving some serious thought to whether we want the lives of our children to be dominated by education in the future and to whether there are alternatives that we should be working toward.

Note on Moral Relativism

Kohlberg, basing his conclusion on some of my earlier writings, has labeled my position one of moral relativism.[1] He sees me, in other words, as holding to a position that rejects any general moral principles and that considers values to be simply a matter of personal taste or group consensus. It should be clear from the preceding overview, and I trust it will be clear to Kohlberg, that this is not my position.

Unfortunately, however, labels have a way of sticking whether they fit or not. Thus it may be worth devoting a few concluding words to the attempt to shed the label of moral relativism. Underlying my whole position on education is the belief that individual freedom should be maximized. I am opposed to public education because I see it as invading the most central area of individual freedom, the freedom to *be* the kind of person one is.

Belief in individual freedom is not a relativistic position, but it tends to look like one. If you believe in individual freedom, you believe in the right of people to act in ways that you would not approve of for yourself. You believe in the right of people to be ignorant, lazy, or promiscuous—even if you have strong personal compunctions against ignorance, laziness, and promiscuity—because you hold as a higher value that these beliefs should not be imposed upon others.

Let us take gambling as an example. In the park across the street from where I live, one may find on any warm day groups of old men clustered around picnic tables, playing cards for money. As it happens I am personally quite opposed to gambling. Yet if I were a parks commissioner I would do nothing to prevent this activity, so long as it did not impinge upon others using the park

[1] Lawrence Kohlberg and Rochelle Mayer, "Development as the Aim of Education," *Harvard Educational Review* 42 (1972): 449–96.

for other purposes. If I were a psychotherapist, I would not try to cure people of the urge to gamble, unless they wanted to be cured. If I were a public school teacher, I would not try to use my public office to shape attitudes against gambling. Yet if I were the director of a community recreation center, I would not allow gambling to go on there. I would tell people that if they wanted to gamble they had better find someplace else to do it. But I would not do that because I wanted to change people according to my own moral principles. I would do it because I cannot see myself presiding over a gambling den. If people didn't like it, they could get rid of me and replace me with someone who did. On the other hand, if people tried to replace me with a recreational director who was dedicated to shaping the character of his clients—who was dedicated, in other words, to education—I would struggle to retain my job and to combat such an anti-libertarian change. For me, therefore, individual freedom is a moral principle that is not simply a matter of personal preference.

Not all societies set great store by individual freedom. The present administration in the United States appears to set less store by it than more liberal administrations of the past. I acknowledge that in states where individual freedom is not a salient value, then public education makes sense. That does not mean, however, that I have a take-it-or-leave-it attitude toward individual freedom. It appears that those who strive to extend individual liberties are always a minority, even in democratic countries. I am with that minority. I believe in the rightness of the struggle to gain greater liberties for the individual, even when the majority of people are opposed to those liberties, as they usually are. I can even conceive of situations where the struggle for liberty could justifiably be carried out by attempting to infiltrate the public schools and to use them for political and propaganda purposes. But this should be recognized as a clear case—in much the same class as fighting a war to achieve peace—of using a dubious means to achieve a worthy end.

I am not trying to say that individual liberty should take precedence over all other values. Much of the analysis in this book is concerned with showing that freedom from public education can be achieved without intolerable sacrifice of other values, such as the values of equal economic opportunity and the material well-being of society. What I want to make clear, however, is that there are definite moral principles underlying my position and that these are not relativistic principles that are simply a matter of personal taste or that apply only to certain societies at certain times.

chapter two

The Search for Morally Acceptable Educational Goals

The first course that prospective teachers usually take is an introduction to education. It is an unpopular course, for its central body of content is a collection of platitudes. One of these platitudes is that society determines the goals of education and the teacher's job is to achieve them. I remember absorbing that principle without question. No one else in my class questioned it either. Yet it is patently false.

Its falsity would have become immediately apparent if someone had asked, "Where does this deciding on the goals of education take place? I would like to go see where it is done." It certainly doesn't go on at school board meetings, which is what the textbook implied. You may find educational goals being discussed in state departments of education, in universities, and in the curriculum offices of local school administrations; but that is not "society" determining goals, it is professional educators doing so. Furthermore the agreed-upon goals are seldom translated into actions that have any influence on what goes on with children in the classroom.

In fact it is local school people, mainly the teachers themselves, who determine educational goals. But *determine* is too positive a word. The actual decisions are of a technical sort—what material to cover, what books to use, what rules to enforce, and so on. The ends toward which these technical decisions are applied are largely unconscious or at least too vague to provide a definite focus for activity.

Yet the responsible teacher does try to educate. She tries to do things that will cause boys and girls to grow up to be a desirable sort of men and women. Where does the teacher get her idea of what is desirable? Well, from any old place, but most likely from the teacher's own upbringing. Thus schooling tends to perpetuate conventional goals. The teacher tends to influence development according to the ideals that were learned in the course of her own development. Little trouble arises from this unless the teacher is confronted with children belonging to a culture with different values or unless the time, like the present, is one of changing values. Then the teacher finds herself bewilderingly out of harmony with her pupils and becomes an enemy force imposing an alien culture.

One remedy is to educate teachers in moral and educational philosophy, to make them conscious and critical of the values they promote. But that is not an acceptable remedy in a free society. If all teachers were philosophers they might be wiser, but this still would not entitle them to determine what kind of people their students should develop into. A wise despot is still a despot.

There is another kind of remedy, however, which lies in trying to set educational goals in a way that does not involve one person deciding what another person should become. A number of possibilities are in the air. I detect eleven of them, which in itself suggests that there must be some widespread, even if unarticulated, concern among educators for shedding the godlike role. Some of the approaches consist merely of ducking the problem, but other more imaginative approaches try to formulate a rationale for discovering goals instead of asserting them. These will deserve serious scrutiny. The labels attached to the various approaches are my own. I am not aware of any other attempts to classify and define them.

1. Liberation goals

The traditional goal of a liberal education is to equip the child to be a free citizen. The term *liberal* in this context means "befitting a free man." The idea is that by equipping a child with skills, knowledge, and the ability to think for himself, you ensure that eventually he will outgrow his teachers and their teachings to become his own kind of person. In American thought Thomas Jefferson was the leading exponent of the idea that education provided a defense against tyranny—not by schooling people in democracy but by producing a citizenry that is competent enough to resist or overthrow tyranny. There is some support for this belief in the history of modern totalitarian regimes, but there is also the counterexample of Nazi Germany. One thing does seem clear and reasonable: teaching people skills renders them potentially more powerful, and a wider distribution of personal power is bound in the long run to work in the interests of freedom. What is more questionable is the effect of education beyond skill training, for when it comes to the development of personality and values it would seem that education can work as easily against as in favor of freedom.

What is wrong with liberation goals is that they can justify almost anything that anyone wants to teach, and indeed they have been so used. Everybody claims to be educating children to be citizens of a democracy. Thus liberation goals are more of an excuse than a guide.

2. Expanded options

We owe to Dewey the method of judging an educational experience according to whether it increases or diminishes the child's capacity for further experience—whether, in other words, it expands or limits his options. Anything you do that increases your competence increases the number of things you can do next. Indoctrination and rigid habit formation close doors on the future.

Dewey's criterion is an appealing one, for it promises a kind of education that would not shape children toward some predetermined end of development. It would not grind out people according to the stereotype of the "good citizen," nor of the rebel or the bohemian or the Renaissance man, either. It would not produce people according to any stereotype at all. By maximizing options it could maximize the possibilities for what each child might become, and thus education would have a maximally unpredictable outcome.

This unpredictability of outcome has been the basis for one objection to Dewey's proposal. What is to prevent the child from growing into a highly competent gangster or corrupt politician? Dewey has replied to this objection, rather unsatisfactorily I think, by suggesting that that kind of growth would shut the individual off "from the occasions, stimuli, and opportunities for continuing growth in new directions."[1] I don't see why. I don't see why the swindler or the graft-taker could not be in a position to grow in as great a variety of ways as the plumber or the philanthropist (there is nothing, in fact, to stop the successful crook from being a philanthropist). Nor do I see why dishonesty is any more limiting than honesty. I would think it might be less limiting.

Another objection has been made by Bertrand Russell. It is that Dewey assumes that unceasing growth is a good thing for everyone. Russell related this assumption to American "boosterism," the belief in the value of unceasing economic growth.[2] Russell's objection was harder to appreciate in the thirties, when he made it, but we can now see what is wrong with continuously accelerating economic growth. Continuously accelerating personal growth still sounds pretty good but, since it is a value that one can live without, to base an educational system on it is to impose a judgment as to what kind of person one should be.

Although the concept of expanded options is different from the concept of liberal education, the two may come to the same thing as regards what is clearly justified and what is questionable. Skills are both liberating and conducive to expanded options. Experiences that form personality and values are questionable according to both criteria. In both cases the educator is called upon to predict long-range effects that he is really in no position to predict. What Dewey has provided is perhaps only a somewhat clearer idea of what liberal education might mean.

3. NATURAL GROWTH GOALS

The study of the normal course of human development has suggested certain universal sequences that are found regardless of cultural differences. Piaget has formulated stages of intellectual growth that have this universality. There is a sensorimotor stage of pre-

[1] John Dewey, *Experience and Education* (New York: Macmillan Co., 1938).

[2] Bertrand Russell, *History of Western Philosophy* (London: Allen & Unwin, 1961), pp. 781–82.

logical function, a stage of concrete operations in which thought is structured after the manner of concrete manipulations of objects, and a stage of formal operations corresponding to mature logical thought. There are substages within each major stage. Development takes place at different rates under different circumstances, but the sequence is claimed to be fixed by the relationship between the organism's structure and that of the environment, and progress is inevitable through all the stages, with the exception that not everyone reaches the final stage.

In recent years informal or child-centered education has been heavily influenced by Piaget's theory. Learning experiences are chosen to fit the child's particular stage of development. In this way, it might seem, educational goals are not invented and imposed on children. Instead the child's needs are discovered by investigation. Thus nature, in a sense, determines the curriculum.

If this child-centered approach were followed strictly, it would amount to teaching only what the child is going to learn anyway. It then becomes questionable what the point is in doing it, and in what sense it is education. In actuality the approach amounts to an informal method of teaching intellectual skills and strategies, with a large emphasis on experimentation. It is far from being culture-free, since it is very much shaped by Western scientific thought, and it leaves the overall development of personality and teaching of values up to the unguided instinct of the teacher. Thus it fails to provide a full basis for educational goals. Furthermore, the approach is mainly applicable to the education of young children, whose cognitive development can be adequately accounted for by a few general trends. It is much less applicable to the education of older children, whose learning branches off into a large number of areas that are each important in their own right.

4. Natural order of values

Kohlberg, who traces his intellectual parentage to both Dewey and Piaget, claims to have discovered a basis for educational goals that transcends cultural differences.[3] His special domain is moral reasoning. He has defined six levels of moral reasoning that range from primitive hedonism through conventional morality to moral judg-

[3] Kohlberg and Mayer, *op. cit.*

ment guided by abstract principles. Unlike Piaget's stages of intellectual growth, Kohlberg's stages are not traversed by all or even most people on their way to adulthood. All six stages are found in adults, although there is a trend toward higher levels of moral reasoning with increasing maturity.

Kohlberg's argument rests not on the universality of progression to higher levels but on the undirectionality of development. Not everyone who reaches level four moves on to level five, but no one moves from level five to level four. Thus the natural course of development provides a clear indication of which way is up. If everyone who reaches level five, which is morality based on social contract, recognizes its superiority to level four, which is morality based on the maintenance of authority, then there is a basis for saying that progress from level four to level five is a good thing—even if those who are stabilized at levels below five do not recognize it. Thus Kohlberg provides a basis for educational intervention that is a good deal bolder than the basis provided by those who adhere only to encouraging the sort of development that occurs naturally in everyone.

Although I am not aware that Kohlberg has done so, similar arguments could be made in areas of taste. In music, for instance, there is a progression in taste from semiclassical to classical music. Not everyone makes it. Many people develop a liking for semiclassical music but never move on to an appreciation of classical music. But no one, it seems, starts out with a liking for Bach and later comes to prefer Rudolph Friml. And so we could use Kohlberg's logic to justify a program of education in music appreciation that was aimed at taking people who like semiclassical music and getting them to appreciate classical music.

Even where there are one-way progressions of a general sort, they are not found in the particulars. There is no one-way progression from Brahms to Beethoven or from Beethoven to Brahms, nor is there one from a belief in monogamy to a belief in free love or the reverse. People's preferences may change in either way. And there are other kinds of value choices that lie outside the main trends altogether. How one feels about rock music, for instance, does not seem to have much to do with where one stands on the semiclassical to classical continuum. It is a horse of another color. The same goes for how one feels about something like abortion: whether one is for it or against it may have little to do with one's level of moral development.

These objections do not invalidate Kohlberg's main point. They only show that his point is limited to very general and abstract characteristics of judgment. Within its limits, Kohlberg's idea has considerable power. What it comes down to, in brief, is that under certain circumstances you can justify imposing changes on people on the grounds that *after* the changes have taken place the people will inevitably see the change as a positive one, even if they were not in a position to see it beforehand.

When the idea is put in these terms, however, we can see its danger. If everyone who became addicted to a drug testified that taking the drug was a good thing, this in itself would not be a convincing argument for inducing everyone to become an addict, for we might say that the addiction was invariably accompanied by a delusion that one was doing the right thing. Yet empirically the case would be the same as movement from level four to level five in moral reasoning: everyone who made the change would count it a change for the better and no one would change back.

In a sense, Kohlberg's criterion of educational good applies, like the other criteria we have considered, only to the acquisition of skills. People who acquire any sort of skill seldom wish the skill away; they find themselves better off having the skill than not having it. And the successively higher levels of moral reasoning are successively higher levels of skill in reasoning—the ability to take more things into account and to see more general patterns in moral problems. There is, in fact, a substantial correspondence between levels of moral reasoning and levels of logical development, as defined by Piaget. Similiarly, we could hold that progression from an appreciation of semiclassical music to an appreciation of classical music is a matter of acquiring ability to discriminate and comprehend the more subtle and complex properties of the latter. Kohlberg, I am sure, would not approve of education that attempted to produce change without the accompanying development of skills. You could indoctrinate people in the theory of social contract, or condition them to respond positively to Brahms and negatively to Friml (with electric shocks and rewards, for instance), but hardly anyone would approve of such "progress." But if skill development is the essential goal, then what we draw from Kohlberg is not a new basis for higher educational goals, but only the identification of an area of skill, in moral reasoning, that had not previously been recognized.

5. Prevailing standards

A traditional basis for justifying educational goals is the prevailing standards of the society. Not everyone may agree as to what honesty is or that honesty according to a certain definition should be taught. However, since the law defines burglary, for instance, as a crime, one may justify teaching children not to commit burglary regardless of how individuals may feel about it. In addition to taking the law as a guide one may also take prevailing standards of decency and social acceptability as a guide for what to teach children. To teach such standards, it may be argued, is not an imposition but rather a natural part of equipping children to function successfully in the society of which they happen to be a part. The fact that other societies or subcultures may have different standards is beside the point.

This approach to defining educational goals stands out from the others because of the level of moral reasoning it represents. To be precise, it represents reasoning at Kohlberg's stage four—reasoning based on the maintenance of law and order. Therein lies its obvious weakness. In contrast to the goals of liberal education, goals based on prevailing standards serve to preserve the status quo rather than to produce citizens who will be in a position to improve upon the existing order. A thinking person might argue that a mixture of the two approaches is desirable, on grounds that education should provide for both continuity and change in society. Such a compromise implies, however, that people in authority will decide on the mixture, on where the balance between continuity and change should be, and even, perhaps, on the specific elements of the status quo to be preserved and those to be changed. Thus this comfortable, middle-of-the-road approach proves on examination not to solve at all the problem of teachers imposing their own goals on children.

6. Democratic goals

A procedural way out of the godlike role of educators is to leave goal-setting in the hands of a democratic process in which citizens or perhaps even the children themselves decide what the goals of education should be. Politically this may be a step away from authoritarianism, but it is no solution to the problem we are treating. At a basic level it does not matter where the goals come from. What matters is whether a minority is forced to accept personal educational goals that are not of their individual choosing.

The issue becomes fuzzier when the process of arriving at educational decisions democratically is thought of as part of the educational process itself, perhaps even its key part. This is the case when teacher-pupil planning becomes a major part of the curriculum or when education is thought to embrace the whole community, so that involving community members in decision-making is treated not merely as the preferred way of determining policy but as a way of educating the community. Then, truly, we may speak of democratic goals rather than democratic procedures for setting goals. It then becomes a little harder to see the forest—the goal—through the procedural trees, but it is still possible to discern that some people are setting out to shape other people to become what the first group wants them to be—in this case, democratic activists.

7. Remedial goals

The model for this kind of goal is medicine. It may be argued that one is not imposing personal goals on others if all one is trying to do is restore them to a state of health. "Getting well" is certainly a natural process—the body is filled with mechanisms for combatting ills and getting itself back to normal. Helping this natural process along is not, therefore, imposing an alien goal on anyone. This argument may be used to justify remedial education for all sorts of exceptional children, as well as to justify a good deal of regular education if it is viewed as remedying some general ailment of the population. Among educators with a psychiatric bent it is common to hear the school spoken of as if it were essentially a psychotherapeutic institution: most children arrive at school as damaged goods and the job of the school is, first of all, not to damage them further, and then to provide a therapeutic milieu in which the children will progress toward mental health.

Although the remedial goal may be fairly clear when the case is one of a broken leg, the cases with which educators deal are never clear. In chapter 4 we shall consider at some length the case of the poor or minority-group child who comes to school with a number of apparent deficits that need treating. It turns out that these are mainly deficits in relation to schooling itself; while "curing" them might enable the child to function better in school, the result might be a child who was even less healthy from any standpoint other than that of the requirements of schooling.

The treatment of perceptual peculiarities and other so-called "learning disabilities" is also, as the latter name implies, a case of treatment for the sake of schooling rather than a case similar to treatment of a broken leg. Such "disabilities" don't handicap the child appreciably outside of school. Indeed they only come to light when children fail to learn to read. A screening of the population of successful children turns up many who have the same "disabilities" but who don't apparently suffer as a result of them. Moreover, even if a perceptual faculty is organically impaired, the educational treatment does not cure it but, at best, enables the child to function scholastically without it.

When it comes to emotional or social problems it becomes even harder to maintain that the therapeutic educator is merely helping nature restore the organism to health. What constitutes mental health is a debatable matter clearly involving personal values. "Adjustment" is good health to some psychologists and subjugation to others. To R. D. Laing schizophrenia is not a disease to be eradicated, but a step in the direction of true sanity.[4]

Far from being morally impeccable, remedial education presents the gravest problems of the educator imposing his own ideas of what other people should be.

8. Compensatory goals

Goals of this kind look rather like remedial goals, but there is an important difference in conceptualization. The emphasis is not

[4] R. D. Laing, *The Politics of Experience* (New York: Pantheon Books, 1967).

on restoring the individual to health but on making up for imbalances in his experiences. The clearest case is physical education. Modern life tends to be sedentary whereas our bodies evolved for an active life of hunting and gathering. Physical education, accordingly, may be viewed not as a way of repairing deficits but as a contrived way of providing some of the physical activity that modern life ordinarily lacks.

By similar reasoning one may justify such things as sensitivity training and encounter groups. For middle-class people, especially, ordinary life emphasizes rationality, inhibition of impulses, and strict adherence to social roles. There has grown up in recent years a vast array of alternative experiences—meditation, sensory awareness activities, nonverbal encounters, and the like—that may be viewed simply as compensating for the one-sidedness of everyday experience. Of course, many people involved in these experiences do not see them as merely compensatory. They see them as changing people and ultimately changing the prevailing way of life. But these experiences can be viewed as merely compensatory, and the question we need to ask is whether from that standpoint they are free from the moral objections that can be made against education generally.

It seems to me that they are free from these objections, providing the experiences are optional ones offered to people capable of making a genuine choice and providing they are offered without some ulterior motive of inducing change in people. They are then, however, no longer what I would call education goals. They are a special variety of what I shall define below as "quality of life" goals.

9. Process goals

A good deal of modern literature on education does not talk at all about changing children but talks about creating a favorable environment for learning and development. I refer to the literature on free schools, open education, child-centered education, and informal education throughout which "imposing" goals is condemned. One has to read this literature carefully, however, for much of it is permeated with educational goals of every sort, and the only thing that distinguishes informal education is the way that the goals are pursued. The teacher does not "impose" his goals in a forthright manner but achieves them deviously through design of the child's environment.[5] The way that goals are pursued is not an issue here, and so when informal education is conceived in this way it solves none of the problems of goal setting at all.

If the child's environment is not designed with some educational intent, then on what basis is it designed? The commonest basis seems to be ideas drawn from developmental psychology about the conditions for healthy child development. Such ideas may, of course, reflect cultural biases and personal values, but it would appear that the educator who tries to limit himself faithfully to creating a healthy, unbiased environment is no more playing god than the cook who tries to provide a healthy diet for a large group of eaters. In the process, however, the educator ceases to be an educator.

10. Quality of life goals

Like pure process goals, these are not educational goals in the true sense, in as much as they do not involve any decisions about what children should become. On the other hand they definitely involve the values of the planner. To pursue an analogy introduced above, the difference between process goals and quality of life goals corresponds to the difference between a cook who merely tries to provide nutritious meals and a cook who aims at getting people to eat well. In the latter case the cook's notions of what constitutes good eating enter much more significantly into the picture, although the difference is only one of degree. The meat-potatoes-and-vegetable cook inevitably imposes a notion of good eating, even if it is a less idiosyncratic one than is imposed by a devotee of *sauce bernaise.*

Since children must be provided for somehow and since the environment in which they function is necessarily largely the creation of adults, there is no escaping the problems associated with imposing on children one's own conception of the good life. These problems are complex enough that a whole chapter (chapter 7) is devoted to them. For the present, however, I will only emphasize that the problems are different from educational problems in that they concern the quality of life for the child in the here-and-now rather than the course of the child's development or its outcome.

[5] Lillian Weber, *The English Infant School and Informal Education* (Englewood Cliffs, N.J.: Prentice-Hall, Inc., 1971), p. 109.

11. Aspirational goals

These are true educational goals, but they are set by the learner, not the teacher. The purest examples of education according to aspirational goals are not found in schools, nor in any other institutions for that matter, but in individual behavioral therapy. Because there is so much misunderstanding of behavioral therapy, I must begin by trying to counteract a stereotype. The common image of behavioral therapy is based on its use in institutions where the unruly child, the lagging worker, or the listless schizophrenic is "shaped up"—usually by a system of rewards—without his consent and sometimes even without his knowledge. From such applications, behavioral therapy has gotten a justifiably bad name as authoritarian and manipulative.

But in individual therapy the situation is quite different. The client tells the therapist how he wants to change. He wants to become more relaxed in talking to groups, he wants to get over a fear of high places, he wants to quit smoking, or he wants to be able to concentrate more on his studies. The therapist merely acts as a technical consultant, helping design a system of contingencies to enable the client to change in the way he wants to change. In this kind of situation the behavioral therapist is, if anything, less authoritarian and manipulative than most other therapists, who are apt to decide that the change the client needs is a different one from the change he wants, and to proceed to work on the client to get him to change in the way that *they* want.

What counts here is not the particular techniques that the therapist uses. They could be of any sort. What counts is the relationship between the goals of the therapist and the goals of the client. Where the goals of the client predominate and are accepted at face value, we have a situation in which education can be carried out without the imposition of one person's values on another. To me this is the only morally acceptable way for public education to be carried out. It presumes, however, that the client or learner is in a position to set his own goals. Thus the approach is only reasonable when the learner has already achieved a certain level of maturity and is able to take a purposeful role in his own development. Such a stage is not normally reached until adolescence. With children, goals may be set by parents. This raises another difficult question of individual rights that will be taken up in the next chapter. Without prejudging that issue, all we can say for now is that aspirational goals appear to solve the moral dilemma of education except in the case of children. And since children are the main concern, we are left, after our examination of eleven possibilities, with no satisfactory solution to the basic dilemma of education.

Morality and the Curriculum

Having considered various nonauthoritarian or apparently non-authoritarian bases for educational goals, let us now take a different tack and look at the elements of a curriculum from the standpoint of their moral implications.

One conclusion to draw from the preceding discussion is that skill training is freer of moral objections than other kinds of teaching. This is a conclusion that many educators find difficult to accept. They are used to thinking of skill training as the most authoritarian part of the curriculum. Perhaps it is, as regards the usual manner of teaching; but we are considering goals, not methods. Skill training can be justified on grounds that in the long run competence serves to liberate the learner from his teachers, as well as from others who have power over him, and it increases the options available to him, thus increasing his freedom.

In order for skill training to have an empowering and liberating effect, however, the skills must be useful. Vocational training teaches skills, surely enough, but it has often been criticized for equipping the learner only to be a cog in the industrial machine or, even worse, for teaching obsolete trades that do not have any value in the job market. As to the first criticism, it is not learning to operate a drill press that condemns a person to life on the assembly line; it is the lack of other skills. But the criticism still has force, because in learning industrial skills the vocational student is spending time and effort that might have been invested in learning other skills (including, for instance, skills in political action) that could free him from a life of drudgery.

Thus, the choice of what skills to teach is significant. Teaching worthless skills is only the extreme case of bad choice of what skills to teach. Difficult choices have to be made all along the line, taking into account not only the potential value of the skills but also the capability of the learner to master them. Perhaps not everyone can profit from training in political debate, but for an educator to make the decision that a particular student cannot profit from such training is rather high-handed.

There are a few skills of undisputed value that are learnable by almost everyone. These are, principally, the three R's of the elementary school. But even they entail important decisions in matters of specific content. Perhaps everyone can profit from learning to read, but should everyone learn to read poetry? Skills in arithmetic generally have obvious practical value, but fractions and negative numbers are very difficult for many children. What good are they, except as a foundation for algebra, and should everyone be expected to learn that? Ability to write increases personal power, but what of all the effort expended on what is generously called "creative writing"? Once we go beyond the three R's we get into even more doubtful cases, the classic one being Latin.

The problem of choice of skills to teach is one that can be solved in a nonauthoritarian manner only by creating a free market in skill learning. A voucher system that offered learners a free choice of publicly available training options would not do the job, because an institution would still be deciding what options to offer. A liberal voucher system that allowed private enterprises into the game, however, would let practical realities of demand take the place of authoritarian decisions.

The question of training methods, which we passed by earlier, is also relevant to value questions. Attitudes and habits may be conditioned in the process of training. Or certain kinds of training may in actuality be available only to people who have suitable attitudes and habits. Again, this consideration argues for a free market, which would be a free market not only in kinds of training but also in methods.

All of the above considerations apply equally to the teaching of knowledge. Knowledge, too, means personal power. The worker may be powerless not only because he lacks political skill but because he lacks knowledge—knowledge of history, knowledge of economics, knowledge even of his own condition, if by that is meant some perspective on it and some awareness of what causes and perpetuates it. But knowledge, too, may vary in usefulness—there are curricular choices to be made—and is susceptible to biases from which skills are comparatively free. Knowledge may be slanted or contrived to favor one kind of behavior and inhibit another. Thus, knowledge may be limiting as well as liberating. That is why sex education, drug education, and religious education are so controversial even when they are carried out in a way that is supposed to be "objective."

Education in the areas of personality and values, as we have seen, is never free of authoritarian imposition. This is distressing because such admirable goals as liberating the individual or increasing his options depend on more than merely teaching skills and knowledge. A person may be skilled and learned and still the prisoner of personal "hang-ups" and narrow attitudes. The only way out that we have seen is through education based on personal goals set by the learner, and such education is accessible only to the older learner, who by that time may already be hardened into his hang-ups and limiting attitudes. But to intervene in the lives of children is to tamper with their personal destinies in a way that only the most arrogant can claim an authority to do.

We are left with the much weaker alternative of merely creating a good environment for children to grow in—and this has its own moral problems associated with it. There is, however, another possibility, little developed at present within the realm of skill training that shows some promise. It is teaching skills within the area generally circumscribed by personality and social behavior.

"Social skills" have an unpleasant connotation. They call to mind such things as salesmanship and leadership training that amount to teaching skills in manipulating other people. A school course in how to be more popular likewise raises the gorge. But recent work in human-relations training has taken quite a different direction. There is such a thing as learning how to speak honestly what is on your mind. There is learning to take the point of view of the other. There is learning to detect game-playing on the part of oneself and others, and learning how to break out of it. There is learning how to express feelings as well as opinions. There is learning how to describe what one sees and hears rather than interpreting on the basis of assumptions. These are all "social skills" but of a nonmanipulative kind. These are skills that many people lack but that most can learn.

I have seen lists of educational objectives that included "emotional skills." The term is nonsense, but there are skills more or less related to emotional and affective life. There are skills of esthetic discrimination, such as being able to tell the difference between a viola and a violin by listening, and being able to recognize the style of a Beethoven or a Hemingway or a Gauguin in an unfamiliar composition. The teaching of such skills does not condition tastes but makes the person capable of developing more differentiated tastes. Some other skills are the ability to recognize when one is in distress; to locate where in the body one feels tension, pain, relaxation, or vigor; to recognize fears, attractions, repulsions, longings, and the like; to tune in or tune out of situations at will and to recognize when one is tuned in or tuned out. These and many related skills are the focus of sensitivity and body awareness training. There may be many more. To acquire such skills is not to become a certain kind of person but rather to acquire a greater capability of becoming the sort of person one desires to be. Present methods of training, such as Gestalt techniques, are not necessarily the best. It has not even been demonstrated beyond doubt that they work. But they do point the way to kinds of skill learning that have not heretofore been considered seriously in our curricula.

Such training should never be other than optional, but I have argued that the same is true for other kinds of training as well. What I am trying to suggest by mentioning these currently faddish kinds of training is that the domain of skill learning is potentially much broader than school curricula indicate. There are manifold ways of increasing personal power and personal options which don't require that we decide in advance what kinds of people children should become.

chapter three

The Right to Make Mistakes

Proposals to do away with compulsory education always sound very attractive if you believe that everyone will turn out better as a result of his new-found freedom. But not everyone will. Some will fritter away their childhoods and later complain that no one made them learn. Some will turn out to be criminals, neurotics, mean sons-of-bitches, and mindless consumers. There will be parents who bar their children from worthwhile learning experiences and force them to spend their days keeping house or being indoctrinated against the evils of communism. Everything bad that can happen to kids will happen to some of them, regardless of whether they are subjected to public education. The sensible thing, therefore, is not to seek perfection but to consider approaches that might, on balance, lead to a somewhat better world than we now have.

But it isn't that easy. There is a perfectionist streak in most of us that will not allow us to tolerate an evil unless we are assured that someone is busy trying to do something about it. The idea that heroin addiction might be reduced by legalizing the sale of heroin wins very few friends, because it would mean *not doing anything* about the addiction that still existed. Similarly, even if the result of abandoning compulsory education was to make most people better off, it would be difficult for many of us to accept a situation in which there were no regulations aimed at doing something about those individuals who were coming to no good. It would seem irresponsible and immoral. "No one," says a recent U.S. Supreme Court decision, "can question the State's duty to protect children from ignorance." [1]

That is hogwash, however. One can very well question the State's duty to protect children from ignorance. This is not to question the value of learning, nor is it to doubt that the state should provide libraries, museums, and other resources for learning. It is to question whether the state has a duty, and consequently a right, to infringe upon the liberty of its citizens in order to ensure that no children grow up in ignorance.

The right of governments to intervene in education seems to be taken for granted everywhere, as if it were as natural a function of a government as maintaining roads. But a little examination will show that there is something fishy about the right of the state to educate:

1. If the state has a right to determine and enforce educational requirements, why does it apply this right only to children? Are there not also ignorant adults? The answer, obviously, is that adults would not stand for compulsory education. Even Hitler and Stalin did not try to make education compulsory for adults, although it seems certain that they would have done so if they had thought they could get away with it. Compulsory education is a terrible affront to individual liberty.

2. By a recent U.S. Supreme Court decision, employers must be prepared to show that any educational requirements they set for employment are relevant to the actual performance of the job.[2] To require arbitrarily that a person have *X* years of schooling to obtain a job is discriminatory. How, then, can the government require *X* years of schooling for everyone—in advance of any knowledge of what kind of job the person will be called upon to perform, and in the absence of any evidence that the schooling equips him with the needed competence?

3. As Everett Reimer has emphasized, school laws and school practices tend to be much the same around the world, regardless of the political systems within which they function.[3] We might

[1] *Wisconsin v. Yoder et al.*, No. 70–110, Supreme Court.
[2] *Griggs v. Duke Power Company*, 91 Supreme Court 849.
[3] Everett Reimer, *School Is Dead* (Garden City, N.Y.: Doubleday & Co., 1971).

suppose, at the very least, there would be a difference in the way education is treated in countries where the individual is subordinated to the state and the way it is treated in those countries where the state is considered to serve the people. The truth seems to be that all governments run their schools as if the individual was the servant of the state. Modern historical analysis suggests that this is not such an unfair judgment and that public education originated as something that the upper classes inflicted upon the lower classes to keep them in line.[4]

Compulsory Training or Compulsory Education?

Although school attendance is required everywhere, we should distinguish between compulsory training and compulsory education. There is some suggestion in a recent U.S. Supreme Court case that such a distinction may come to be recognized in the courts. The case involved Amish parents who refused on religious grounds to send their children to high school. One of the reasons brought forth by the Supreme Court in favor of the parents was that

> *When Thomas Jefferson emphasized the need for education as a bulwark of a free people against tyranny, there is nothing to indicate he had in mind compulsory education through any fixed age beyond a* basic *education* [*emphasis added*].[5]

In footnotes to this quotation it is made explicit that what Jefferson had in mind as basic education was training in the "three R's." Since the Amish children do acquire such basic learning, and since they have a long record of successful social functioning, then for such children, says the Court

> *there is at best a speculative gain, in terms of meeting the duties of citizenship, from an additional one or two years of compulsory formal education.*[6]

[4] Michael Katz, *Class, Bureaucracy, and Schools: The Illusion of Educational Change in America* (New York: Praeger, 1971); Marvin Lazerson, *The Origins of the Urban School* (Cambridge, Mass.: Harvard University Press, 1971); and Jonathan Messerli, *Horace Mann: A Biography* (New York: Alfred A. Knopf, 1972).

[5] *Wisconsin v. Yoder et al.*

[6] *Ibid.*

Now certainly there is at best a speculative gain for everything that is taught in the schools beyond the basic skills. If the state can demand only that children submit to instruction that is of some demonstrated benefit it seems eventually it must demand only that children receive training in the three R's.

While compulsory training in the three R's strikes me as unsavory, I do not see it as inconsistent with the character of a liberal democracy. It is in much the same class as compulsory military training. It involves acquiring certain minimum skills for what is deemed to be the good of society. The critical question is whether the need is sufficient to justify the imposed duty. When the answer is yes—as it is in Israel, for instance, with regard to military preparedness—then even the most libertarian of people are likely to agree that the state has a right to demand such training. The value of literacy to a society is obvious enough. In countries where illiteracy is a substantial obstacle to social betterment, I think the nation would have full right to make training compulsory. In the wealthy nations, however, where illiteracy is already rare and where the value of literacy is appreciated by one and all, it seems difficult to justify imposing literacy training as a civic duty.

If a government made basic skill training freely available and issued certificates of competence in each skill at various levels of attainment, then I think the practical need for compulsion would vanish. Realistic job requirements would provide sufficient motive to seek training. I would emphasize, however, that the issue of compulsory basic skill training involves a practical question of whether a genuine need for it exists and whether the need would actually be better met by compulsory training or by some other approach. It does not involve the fundamental question of whether or not the state has a right to require such a thing.

Compulsory *education* is another story altogether. It is not at all evident that the state has any business meddling in the formation of character and beliefs. In determining that schools could not compel children to salute the flag, the U.S. Supreme Court declared that to force such an expression of belief would be to invade "the sphere of intellect and spirit which it is the purpose of the First Amendment to our Constitution to reserve from all official control." [7] But surely anything that deserves the name of

[7] *Board of Education v. Barnette,* 319 U.S. Supreme Court 624.

education must involve some penetration into "the sphere of intellect and spirit."

The dubious position of education is shown rather strikingly in regard to religious education. In the United States the government and the public schools must scrupulously avoid religious education because of the First Amendment prohibition against the establishment of a state religion. In England, on the other hand, religious instruction is *required* by law, and apparently is considered by many educators to be of the highest importance in fulfilling the educational function of the schools.[8]

Many American educators must feel the same way, considering the lengths to which they have gone to sneak religious education into the schools in spite of all the prohibitions against it. (Whether religious education actually is important in the development of character and attitudes needn't concern us here; it is sufficiently to the point that many people on both sides of the Atlantic think it is.)

How could two nations so closely related culturally end up at opposite poles on a matter such as this? Not because of a major difference in educational philosophy, obviously, but because of a political difference in the handling of relations between church and state. The result, however, is that the United States is in a most anomalous position, where its Supreme Court may declare on the one hand that "education is perhaps the most important function of state and local governments," and on the other hand forbid those governments to have anything to do with what many people consider to be the heart of personal development. The English are more consistent, but at the price of what liberal Americans would consider an intolerable disregard of freedom of belief.

Finally we can disentangle religion from the totality of personal values and beliefs only by arbitrary or doctrinaire definitions. This has come to be recognized in regard to conscientious objection to military service. At one time conscientious objectors had to demonstrate longtime membership in a recognized pacifist religious sect. Now the U.S. courts allow that "a sincere and meaningful belief" may qualify as religious under the First Amendment guar-

[8] Nan Berger, "The Child, the Law and the State," in *Children's Rights,* ed. J. Hall (London: Elek Books, 1971), pp. 153–79.

antees of religious freedom, even though not based on the teachings of a sect or on a belief in a deity, if it occupies a central place in the life of the possessor.[9] If this broad notion of "religious" is applied to education, so that public schools are barred from tampering with any "sincere and meaningful belief," it would obviously become impossible for the schools to do anything that deserved the name of education.

Eventually, I think, the courts will be driven to honor parental objections of conscience and religion that apply to anything taught in public schools beyond the basic scholastic skills. I have already pointed out indications of such a tendency in the recent Supreme Court decision concerning the Amish. Dating from farther back is the opinion of a Supreme Court that

> *No pupil attending the school can be compelled to study any prescribed branch against the protest of the parent that the child shall not study that branch, and any rule or regulation that requires the pupil to continue such studies is arbitrary and unreasonable.*[10]

(This principal, incidentally, has been invoked to exempt pupils from studying such noncontroversial subjects as grammar.)

Of course, anyone who doesn't like what the public schools do or propose to do with his children's minds has an out. He can send his children to a private school. The fact that private schools are permitted stands as a tacit admission that public education is a threat to individual liberty. When the State of Oregon, back in the twenties, tried to require all children to attend public schools it was slapped down by the U.S. Supreme Court with the stern words that follow:

> *The fundamental theory of liberty upon which all governments in this Union repose excludes any general power of the State to standardize its children by forcing them to accept instruction from public school teachers only. The child is not the mere creature of the State. . . .*[11]

Given such an admission, however, it is not much of a compensation to allow parents to send their kids to private schools. Private schools almost always involve extra costs to the users. Furthermore,

[9] *United States v. Seeger,* 380 U.S. Supreme Court 163.
[10] *Meyer v. Nebraska,* 262 U.S. Supreme Court 390.
[11] *Pierce v. Society of Sisters,* 268 U.S. Supreme Court 510.

because public schools deliver training and education in a package deal, parents who don't want the education for their children—who object to it on religious, political, or moral grounds—have to forego the free public training as well. That is clearly discriminatory—as if in order to go to a public park you had to eat the hot-dogs served there, thus denying use of the park to orthodox Jews, Moslems, and other non-pork eaters.

Four Conceptions of the Child

When viewed with a little detachment, public education—especially compulsory education—is seen to be preposterous and out of keeping with notions of human rights and the sanctity of the individual. Yet public education is almost universally accepted no matter how much people might object to particular ways of carrying it out. How is it to be justified? The reasons for public education come very readily to mind. There is no use merely listing them. But perhaps we can put them into an intelligible framework by considering four different views of children—most people, I suppose, hold all four at the same time.

1. THE CHILD AS A SOCIAL PRODUCT

Although a particular Mommy and Daddy create and typically raise each child, the rearing of children may be considered a function of the whole society. Surely it is a legitimate concern of the whole society. To view children as social products is to view them as part of a society's effort to perpetuate and advance itself. According to this viewpoint, the rearing of children by their natural parents is one alternative which might be supplanted by a better one, such as the kibbutz model. Parents are not viewed as having any unchallengeable right to determine how their children shall be raised. Kids may be taken from parents who aren't adequately serving society's purposes or parents may be compelled to follow rules such as bringing their children in for health checks or sending them to schools. Compulsory parent education may be a reasonable possibility. A further step might be to license couples to have children. Ultimately the view of children as social products would lead one to favor compulsory eugenics, so that only those children who had a better-than-average chance of being social assets would be born. I don't mention eugenics invidiously. It seems to me to be a natural and perfectly reasonable conclusion from the same arguments that would lead one to favor compulsory education for the good of society.

2. The child as an extension of his parents

Underlying this view is the fact that people's values and aspirations are often profoundly tied up with their children. If you allow parents to practice any religion they please but forbid them to raise their children in that religion, you make a travesty of religious liberty. If you bar children from certain movies you limit the right of parents to expose their children to experiences they deem valuable. If you require school attendance or education of any kind you limit parental freedom of belief and action. In the extreme, this view sees the child as nothing more than a small walking embodiment of parental interests, sometimes of the most admirable sort, sometimes not.

3. The child as a ward

This view stresses the helplessness of children and the fact that, in part at least, someone else must look after their interests. Parents are seen as having a duty to care for their children and provide for their futures, but society has a duty to move in where parents are not sufficient. Laws pertaining to children—such as child labor laws and compulsory school attendance laws—are needed because parents and other people cannot always be trusted to do what is best for children.

4. The child as a citizen

When the child is considered as a person in his own right, then it is seen that his freedoms are infringed upon both by compulsory schooling and by the authority of parents to control his behavior. This view of the child is occasionally given pious assent, but little is ever done in keeping with it. Most people who talk about the rights of children will be found to be talking about the child as a ward rather than the child as a citizen.

In a very interesting philosophical analysis of the right to educate, Francis Schrag observes that all three of the parties we have been considering—society, parents, and the child—have a legitimate interest in how children are educated.[12] Schrag concludes that there is no neat way of resolving their possibly conflicting interests and that the wisest allocation of rights may differ from one situation to another. Where the survival of a subculture is at stake, Schrag favors the right of parents to decide how they want their children to be brought up, but under more normal conditions he would "support efforts to undermine the tyranny which individual parents exert over their children." [13]

Schrag, it seems, is looking at the child mainly as a social product. His concern is that the product shouldn't be excessively standardized. I think a good deal of literature on child-centered education is written from the same standpoint, that allowing diversity creates a better social product.

While I would agree that society, parents, and children all have a legitimate interest in how children are raised, I would argue that the interests of each are different and that lines can therefore be drawn between them. Society's *legitimate* interest in child-rearing is, it seems to me, a very limited one. The interest is essentially the same as people's interest in the character of their neighbors and fellow townsfolk. Given a choice of neighbors, some fairly standard criteria would probably emerge: honesty, responsibility, lawfulness, self-sufficiency, etc. But people do not actually have any choice that is protected by law. The idea of the residents of a city forcing would-be residents to pass entrance examinations is repugnant, for it gives an unwarranted authority to the people who happen already to be there. A city has to make do with the people who want to live there, which seems only reasonable since the city essentially *is* the people who choose to live there.

What is true of the people who move into a city from the countryside is true of the people who move into it from the maternity

[12] Francis Schrag, "The Right to Educate," *School Review* 79 (1971): 359–78.
[13] *Ibid.*, p. 376.

author is citing problems stemmed basic from Human Society not education Solution would mean change of culture.

wards: they have a right to be there; they shouldn't have to meet standards. But somehow it has gotten established that the older generation, merely by virtue of being there first, has a right to determine what the incoming generation should be like in order to be satisfactory as citizens, and to force education upon them to make them become that way. This strikes me as plain arrogation, accomplished only because the incoming generation lacks the power to object.

People are not, of course, powerless to do anything about their neighbors. In addition to informal means of influence and selection, which they can apply to children as well, they may have recourse to law if their neighbors cause or threaten damage to them. I suggest a similar limitation of their legal right to impose education on other people's children: where a child is causing harm or presenting a clear and present danger of doing harm, then society should be able to take action, which may consist of compulsory education. It should, of course, only be applied to individuals and only by due legal process.

The interest that parents have in the rearing of their own children is of a wholly different kind, going much deeper. The difficulty, indeed, is that the legitimate parental interest in children is essentially limitless. You cannot tell parents they have a legitimate interest in some aspects of their children's development but not in others. Their legitimate interest embraces the whole child. Nor can you say, your legitimate interest extends only until the child is so many years old, since conditions are not radically altered by the occurrence of a birthday.

According to the U.S. Supreme Court,

> [a] *State's interest in universal education, however highly we rank it, is not totally free from a balancing process when it impinges on other fundamental rights and interests, such as . . . the traditional interest of parents with respect to the religious upbringing of their children. . . .*[14]

Surely that statement has the priorities all backward. Society's interest in the child as a future citizen is relatively insignificant compared to the parents' interest not only in the religious upbring-

[14] *Wisconsin v. Yoder et al.*

ing of their children but in all aspects of their upbringing. It is the parents' interest, in fact, that may not be "totally free from a balancing process." And at that, the interest that needs to be balanced against the parents' interest is not that of the state but rather that of the children themselves.

The child has a legitimate interest in his own upbringing that runs at least as deep and extends at least as far as his parents' interest, and ultimately it should have priority. The real problem, therefore, in settling the issue of the right to educate, is to balance parents' rights against children's rights. This is a problem made exceedingly difficult because of the fact that at the outset the child is in no position to assert rights of his own.

The state looks after children's welfare to a limited extent. In extreme cases of cruelty or neglect the state steps in to punish parents or to remove the child. The courts are notoriously reluctant to act against parents in such cases, but in cases where they haven't been so reluctant to act for the child's welfare, the results have been scandalous. Children have been snatched away from their natural parents because a judge found the parents too unconventional in their style, not properly church-going, or, most recently, not possessed of a satisfactorily high IQ. These are the cases that get in the news, of course, but they demonstrate that as soon as the state goes beyond dealing with the most obvious mistreatments of children it encroaches gravely upon the civil liberties of parents.

Compulsory education may be viewed as an indirect way of protecting the child's rights. That must be how the framers of the Universal Declaration of Human Rights saw it. I don't know any other basis on which sane men could have included in a list of human *rights,* the statement, "Elementary education shall be compulsory."

What this "right" amounts to, as far as the child is concerned, is that he has two masters instead of one and thus is assured of a more balanced treatment. His parents may have fanatical ideas about how he should be raised or they may be drunken brawlers who hit him every time he crawls out from behind the couch. By requiring that the child spend his days in a state-approved school the state automatically moderates such extreme treatments.

There is a certain reasonableness to this justification for compulsory education. It is the justification that most liberal adults give me. However, it is not the justification that the courts give, and it is very doubtful if compulsory education could stand up in court if it were justified only on grounds that it protected the rights of the child. After all, there are children who are poorly fed but we don't, because of that, require all children to take their meals in public dietary kitchens. Instead we try to help and convince parents to feed their children better, and use the law only to deal with extreme cases. It would be hard to justify protecting children from ignorance with measures more severe than we use to protect them from starvation.

If there were no compulsory education in America, how many children would be prevented by their parents from obtaining the learning that was in their best interests? We don't know, of course, and that in itself is a strike against the defenders of compulsory education. A reasonable supposition is that the number would be quite small—too small to justify compulsory schooling for the millions, and probably smaller than the number of children who are now prevented by the compulsory education laws from obtaining the learning that is in their best interests.

In conclusion, we find that educational policy in the modern world is primarily based on a view of the child as a social product, with a nod toward the view of the child as an extension of his parents. There is also some recognition of the child as a ward, whose interests must be protected for him by the state. What we do not find is any recognition of the child as a citizen, entitled to exercise rights of his own. Yet if there is to be any effective and legitimate balance against the tyranny of parents, it is not going to come from the state acting in its own or the child's behalf. It is going to have to come from the child, empowered with rights he doesn't currently have. What should those rights be, and how can the child be empowered with them? These questions, I think, define the next frontier in the struggle for human rights.

The Frontier of Children's Rights

In the case of *Wisconsin* v. *Yoder,* in which Amish parents challenged the compulsory schooling laws of Wisconsin, Justice William O. Douglas delivered a partially dissenting opinion. He dissented on the grounds that two of the three children involved had not been consulted as to what they themselves thought about going to high school. Said Justice Douglas:

> *If the parents in this case are allowed a religious exemption, the inevitable effect is to impose the parents' notions of religious duty upon their children. Where the child is mature enough to express potentially conflicting desires, it would be an invasion of the child's rights to permit such an imposition without canvassing his views.*[15]

"This issue has never been squarely presented before today," Justice Douglas observed. Unfortunately the court decided the issue was not relevant to the case, and so the rights of children against their parents have not yet had their day in court.

The status of children is rather similar to that of slaves and women in times past: they have no rights of their own and are assumed not to need any because they are in the care of a master who is expected to exercise his own rights benevolently in their behalf. The awarding of rights to children, however, presents difficulties far exceeding those of awarding rights to slaves and to women. Although in the latter cases there was some doubt as to whether those concerned were competent to exercise their rights, in the case of children there is no doubt that every child begins life in a state of incompetence. Thus, at least at the beginning, someone must act as the trustee of his rights, and so the question of how and when and by what criteria the child is to assume the rights for himself is inevitable. Would Justice Douglas have been so concerned about respecting the children's desires if they had been eight years old instead of fourteen? Would he have been so concerned if it had been a case in which the parents wanted the children to go to school but the children, more orthodox than their parents, had objected to school on religious grounds?

Children's rights have become a popular topic for radical thinkers. The literature of educational radicalism is shot through with assertions of children's natural rights. A book has recently been published, and now a journal devoted to children's rights.[16] And yet I have not seen any serious, constructive attempt to deal with

[15] *Ibid.*

[16] Julian Hall, ed., *Children's Rights* (London: Elek Books, 1971). The journal bears the same name.

the problem of how rights can be turned over to children—how, that is, the transition is to be made from the totally dependent status of infancy to the autonomous status of full citizenship.

There do not seem to be a very large number of possibilities. You could give full rights to children at birth and leave it up to the natural process of development to determine when the child would begin to start asserting them. That does not strike me as a very good idea. Politicians might find it too easy to buy a six-year-old's vote—nor is the prospect of a ten-year-old being cheated out of all his worldly goods by a fast-talking twelve-year-old very attractive. Another is to set an arbitrary age for accession to full rights. That is where we are now. Moving the age down to fourteen would solve a lot of problems, and might on balance be the wisest solution. Another is to set the automatic age for accession to full rights rather high—at eighteen or twenty-one as is done now—but to allow for special pleas in court at younger ages whereby a child might claim certain rights against the wishes of his parents. This has the appeal of rationality, but on the other hand would be very complicated to administer, would tend to favor only the most sophisticated children, and would have the unpleasant effect of setting parents and children into an adversary relationship, the ill effects of which are notoriously demonstrated by the divorce courts.

It would be presumptuous of me to propose a solution, since I have not the legal knowledge to be aware of the complications involved. For the present topic, however, we don't have to consider all the rights and privileges of citizenship, but only one. Let us put the question concretely: Suppose that there is a voucher system for use of learning resources. Who decides how the child's vouchers should be spent, the child or his parents? Assuming that for very young children the answer is that the parents decide, then how and when is the authority transferred to the child? I believe we can answer questions of this kind without having, at the same time, to settle when children should be free to marry, vote, or purchase automobiles without parental consent.

I see two reasonable answers to the voucher question. One is that the parents decide how the vouchers are to be used until the child is eighteen years old, except that a child may at any time appeal to a court of children's rights where he might present his own proposal for use of the vouchers, where the parents could present counterarguments, and where a judicial process would then decide whether the child should at that time be granted autonomy, not in all things, but in the specific matter of choice of his own learning experiences. I have already indicated the drawbacks of this approach.

The other approach would be to establish by law that children at age thirteen or fourteen could enter into agreements for the use of learning vouchers, in other words that they would be free to use them as they wished without parental endorsement. This would not end parental authority in other areas but it would end it in an area that is central to the child's development as an autonomous human being. It would not, of course, end parental influence. Parents certainly have a strong interest in what happens to their children educationally after the age of thirteen. It only means that parents would have to work through persuasion and through what they had been able to instill in their children during the preceding thirteen years, rather than through arbitrary authority.

I choose the age thirteen simply because it seems to be an age around which children typically begin to take an interest in their own development—in personal learning as well as in acquiring an organized knowledge of the world and a set of belief's about significant issues. While it is true that not all children acquire such interests then (some of them may never do so) and that some children acquire them earlier (very few, in my experience), I don't see any great amount of injustice or misfortune following from awarding at age thirteen the right to direct one's own learning.

The Right to Make Mistakes

Should people—should children in particular—have the right to make mistakes? That is the question that was raised at the beginning of this chapter, and it remains as a basic question after we have considered possibilities of taking educational authority away from the state and placing it in the hands of parents and children. My impression is that virtually every educator, every social worker, most psychologists and psychiatrists, in short, almost everyone in the "helping" professions operates on a deeply-rooted conviction that people should not be allowed to make mistakes. Even most educational radicals have this belief, but rationalize their way around it by entertaining the optimistic belief that if you let everyone follow their natural impulses, no one will make mistakes.

Now of course teachers, school administrators, counsellors, and other protectors of the incompetent also make mistakes, and it could be argued that on balance the mistakes people would make with their own lives would be less costly. But that argument readily leads to the conclusion that the thing to do is improve the quality of the various guidance services. What it comes down to in the end is this: if you grant someone a right you grant him the opportunity to make mistakes. If you grant someone the right to determine his own course of development you grant him the right to become miseducated or the right not to be educated at all. A right is something that a person is entitled to whether he uses it wisely or not.

Scenarios for the abuse of educational freedom are easy to write. Here is Sally H., born to an incompetent unmarried mother on welfare. Because mother typically sleeps till noon, Sally misses out on most of the normal learning experiences of early childhood. By age thirteen she is virtually illiterate, defensive about it, drops out of all organized youth activities, and spends her days in various delinquent activities with a gang of similar teenagers. Here is George M. whose mother is determined he shall be the world's greatest accordion player, keeps him out of most other learning activities so that he can practice ten hours a day. At age fifteen George throws his accordion out the window and takes to the road as a drifter. Here is Ram D. whose parents have him into Zen and peyote by age ten. By age seventeen he is big on staring into water drops and good at stitching leather, but devoid of most of the skills that would enable him to get into architecture, for which he has acquired a great passion. Here is Jeffry B., carefully steered by his parents throughout childhood into activities that develop his very obvious academic talents. But at thirteen Jeffry exercises his right to abandon all of that in favor of rock music, has a good time playing the guitar for about five years, but never gets good enough at it to make a living. He gives it up when he gets a job as a maintenance worker in an office building.

Obviously such children are found today, the Sally H.'s in great number. It is quite possible that their numbers would be no greater if the state relinquished its control over education. But the question remains, shouldn't something be done to prevent such misfortunes, such a waste of childhood potential, such human ruin? Assuredly so, but through influence, as one would influence others to eat better or to quit smoking, and not, I think, through authority. The exception might be Sally H.: there are parents who fail drastically to carry out their responsibilities, and there needs to be a legal process for stepping in. But for the rest, no. I have written scenarios of failure, but they might have been successes. George M. might have become the world's greatest accordionist and enjoyed it; Ram D. might have turned out to be one of the few people psychologically equipped to live in the 1980's, thanks to the unconventional foresight of his parents; Jeffry B. might have decided at thirteen to forge ahead with his scholarly studies, or have gone back to them with little loss after a joyous interlude as a musician. It is not, I submit, the business of any authority to determine that children shall have this and that learning experience and not some other. Even if the authorities could make wiser decisions most of the time (which I doubt would be true in practice), it is not their business to do so. Certainly there are experts who could make wiser decisions about how we ought to spend our money than most of us can. If we care to we can hire their services. But who would give them the power to determine how we spend our money? Who would empower a ministry of culture to compel us to spend our leisure time in approved ways? Our lives, if we examine them closely, are compounded of innumerable mistakes that are the price we gladly pay for the privilege of being free. Not a few of these mistakes are ones for which our children too must pay the price.

chapter four

Is Inequality Here to Stay?

The moral dilemma in education comes out most clearly in the education of poor people. Wealthy people can by-and-large get the kind of education for their children that they want. They wield considerable influence over the schools, and if they can't get the public schools to provide what they want they can pay to send their children elsewhere. Poor people have to take what is offered and so they are continually at the mercy of educators who think they know what is best for other people's children.

One of the commonest arguments against turning educational decisions over to parents and children is that the poor would not know how to make use of such freedom. They would make mistakes, give their children an inferior kind of education, and thus perpetuate the "cycle of poverty."

This fear sounds reasonable, but there is no satisfactory evidence to support it. The most pertinent evidence has been analyzed by Jencks and his colleagues in their book, *Inequality*.[1] They have looked at the effects of schooling and family background on various measures of success. Occupational status appears to be the most predictable measure of success. There is a considerable tendency for occupational status to be passed on from generation to generation. When occupations are rated on a 96-point scale, it is found that

[1] Christopher Jencks et al., *Inequality: A Reassessment of the Effect of Family and Schooling in America* (New York: Basic Books, 1972).

fathers whose occupations differ by 60 points have sons whose occupations differ by about 30 points in status. Jencks *et al.* calculate that about half of this 30-point advantage can be attributed to differences in amount of schooling, independent of any differences in amount of ability.

One can read these results as showing that schooling is an important determinant of the occupational level a person will attain, and that high-status people pass on their advantages to their children in substantial part through schooling. Thus, it may be argued, if you want poor children to have a chance to improve their status, you had better see that they get as much schooling as children of the rich.

Jencks finds, however, that quality of schooling has almost nothing to do with occupational status. From all appearances it is not what is learned at school but simply the fact of having gone through it that opens the doors to higher occupational status. Indeed, Jencks calculates that if occupational status were awarded on the basis of ability rather than schooling, this would tend to *reduce* inequality due to family background.

Thus, further analysis reveals that schooling, under the present conditions of society, should not be viewed as an equalizer but as a preserver of differences in social status. If schooling itself were no longer a credential for employment and if people were free to develop their capabilities as they saw fit, there is reason to believe that children of the poor would, on the whole, have a better rather than worse chance to rise in the occupational hierarchy.

A more general conclusion from Jenck's study, however, is that nothing that can be done with education can be expected to have a very marked effect on inequality. If social equality is a serious goal, it will have to be pursued through more direct means, such as through direct efforts to equalize incomes and to reduce the privileges associated with high-status occupations.

Skill Deficiencies

Anyone who has been close to the education of poor children cannot escape the impression that Jenck's statistical analyses brush an important problem under the rug. Jencks is aware that lower-class children do not achieve as well in school as middle-class children. His point, and it is a very significant one, is that this fact does not go very far toward explaining why some people are poor and others are rich. School achievement and IQ (which is primarily a predictor of school achievement) do not begin to account for the variation in occupational status and income that may be observed in modern societies.

Nevertheless, school learning has some significance in its own right, quite apart from its economic value. We do not need statistics to convince us that it is better to be literate than illiterate, better to be knowledgeable than ignorant, better to be mathematically competent than incompetent. On all of these counts it is quite clear that lower-class children fare much worse than middle-class children in today's schools. One can cite achievement test data to show that in twelve years of schooling lower-class children learn only as much as middle-class children learn in nine. Such data are questionable, because achievement tests largely measure intellectual aptitude rather than learning itself. The truth could be either better or worse, but no one questions that lower-class children generally come out of school with less of the knowledge and skills that schools are supposed to impart.

Our question is, can anything be done about this condition, and, if so, will it require more or less imposition of educational goals on poor children? To answer this question we must start with causes. What accounts for the lower achievement of poor children?

Two main kinds of explanation are now vying with each other. They are called, in rather loaded terms, the "deficit" explanation and the "difference" explanation. The deficit explanation holds that poor children, because of environmental conditions and possibly because of heredity, are lacking in some of the traits necessary for successful school learning. The difference explanation holds that poor children, particularly poor black Americans, are not deficient in any basic way but have cultural differences that are not appreciated by the schools. These differences lead on one hand to the *appearance* of deficits on intelligence and language tests and on the other hand to learning difficulties arising from the fact that schools are designed for and operated by middle-class people.

To a considerable extent the deficit explanation and the difference explanation say the same thing in different words. What both are saying is that lower-class children have differences in language, background knowledge, and dispositions that put them at a disadvantage in school. What is controversial is the claim, made by a number of radical social scientists who have rallied around the difference explanation, to the effect that, if lower-class children were tested fairly and exposed to education sensitive to their cultural differences, they would do as well as anyone else.

If it could be verified that with a different form of education lower-class children would achieve as well as middle-class children, then we would not have to worry about the issue of test-score differences. Test scores are only of interest as predictors of achievement.

To date, however, I do not know of any demonstrated educational approaches that eliminate social class differences in the learning of intellectual skills. There are approaches, that I will discuss later, which promise to raise the achievement of lower-class children considerably, but they do not remove differences. They also raise the achievement of middle-class children. Furthermore, among the kinds of educational approaches currently being tried in the Follow-Through programs, the ones that have been succcessful in raising achievement are those that make no particular concessions to cultural differences but that concentrate on efficient training techniques. The possibility remains that more radical adaptations to cultural differences will tell another story, but in the meantime we are compelled to look at test scores and what they mean.

The question that radical social scientists have asked—Are poor kids really deficient or are they only different?—has been asked in much too narrow a context. They have asked, are poor kids really deficient in intelligence or language skills? Faced with the evidence of low scores on intelligence and language tests, the "difference" advocates proceed to explain these differences away. The kids speak a different dialect; they aren't used to taking tests; the testers frighten them; testers don't give them enough time and lower-class kids lack the middle-class kids' penchant for speedy response; they aren't as competitive; the tests demand conventional, conforming responses, thus handicapping the child who is different; lower-class kids aren't interested in the artificial tasks presented by tests; and so on. Evidence is adduced to show that when these conditions are changed—when the children are given more time and encouragment, or when language is assessed by more informal means—poor kids make a better showing.[2]

Fine, but all of this is beside the point if you are concerned with the children's chances for school success. For in relation to school success the child's understanding of Standard English, his competitiveness, his willingness to pursue artificial tasks, and so on, are all part of the package. They are not "noise" to be filtered out in order to get a true reading of the child's scholastic aptitude. It does no particular good to demonstrate that by making testing conditions more favorable for the child in every way you can get a higher test score out of him if his original, lower test score is the one that best predicts how he will do in school.

To get the facts fully straightened out, however, we have to recognize further that the "difference" advocates have not actually succeeded in explaining away IQ and language deficits on tests. It is no news that such things as motivation, test-wiseness, and familiarity with the language can have an effect on test performance. The question is how much effect. Is it enough to account for the discrepancy in scores between middle-class and lower-class children? In testing the IQs of young children who have never before been in school, it appears that a gain of from 4 to 6 IQ points can be achieved among lower-class children simply by giving them a few weeks of experience in a Head Start program or by testing them under more favorable conditions. Middle-class children don't show such a gain, and so some of the difference in IQ can probably be attributed to various factors influencing the child's adaptation to test-like situations. But lower-class children don't show additional gains except when substantial learning goes on, and most of the data on social-class and ethnic differences in mental abilities are from children who have been in school for some time. The difference amounts to around 15 IQ points when lower-class black children are compared with middle-class whites.

There have been several careful experiments that should have reduced this 15-point difference if the "difference" theorists are right, but they haven't succeeded. Several studies have looked at what happens when lower-class black children are tested with standard IQ tests administered by black testers speaking the child's own

[2] Herbert Ginsburg, *The Myth of the Deprived Child* (Englewood Cliffs, N.J.: Prentice-Hall, Inc., 1972).

dialect.[3] The children essentially did no better. Of course, the problem could be in the tests themselves. Jensen and Fredriksen carried out an ingenious experiment that controls for all the factors that might enter into the testing experience itself.[4] It was a simple test of recall. Children were shown twenty different objects and then asked to recall as many of them as they could. The test was given in two forms that were identical as to what was done with the children. In the "uncategorized" version the twenty objects did not fall into any obvious classes or groupings. In the "categorized" version, the twenty objects were selected so that they fell into several groups. The report doesn't indicate what the groups were—presumably such things as animals, tools, etc. The objects were mixed up, however, so that the tools, for instance, were not all grouped together. Scores on the "uncategorized" version showed little or no correlation with IQ, while scores on the "categorized" version showed substantial correlation with standard IQ measures. Apparently, then, high-IQ children were able to make use of the groupings of objects as an aid to memory.

When middle-class white children were compared with lower-class black children on these two versions of the memory test, it was found that they did about equally well on the "uncategorized" version, but the middle-class white children scored a standard deviation higher than the lower-class black children on the "categorized" IQ-related version. A standard deviation difference corresponds to about 15 points of IQ, the difference found on ordinary IQ measures.

The impressive thing about this experiment is that any of the factors that the "difference" theorists might appeal to as explanations of low performance—motivation, fear of the tester, meaninglessness of the task, etc.—should apply equally well to both versions of the test. The differences in performance between the two tests could only be due to differences in what the children were able to

[3] J. M. Sattler, "Racial 'Experimenter Effects' in Experimentation, Testing, Interviewing, and Psychotherapy," *Psychological Bulletin,* 73 (1970): 137–60; Lorene C. Quay, "The Effects of Language and Reinforcement on the Intelligence Test Performance of Negro Children," *Child Development,* 42 (1971): 5–15.

[4] A. R. Jensen and Janet Fredriksen, "Social Class Differences in Free Recall of Categorized and Uncategorized Lists," in *Experimental Analysis of Learning Abilities in Culturally Disadvantaged Children,* ed. A. R. Jensen and W. D. Rohwer, Jr. (Final report on OEO Project No. 2404, U.S. Office of Economic Opportunity, 1970), pp. 103–18.

make of the information provided for them. Dialect differences could not enter in either, because the children were not required to name the categories of objects. It would not matter in the least if the children used labels from a nonstandard dialect or used no labels at all, so long as they were able to make use of the logical organization of the set of objects.

This evidence is perhaps a bit esoteric, but such evidence is needed if one is to clear away the uncertainties surrounding differences in performance on standardized tests. Regular tests always allow for conflicting explanations of the differences in scores between groups. Given the experimental evidence, however, it appears reasonable to hold that there are genuine differences in mental abilities that are relevant to the different scholastic performance of middle-class and lower-class children. The causes of the differences remain open to speculation, but it seems clear that they are not just an illusion created by the injustices of mental testing.

We should not make the mistake of putting all the emphasis on IQ differences, however. IQ is undoubtedly important as a predictor of school achievement, but it tends to be overrated in that respect and overrated even more as a predictor of success in other walks of life. Interest, motivation, and temperament are also important factors in school learning, and in these poor children are also at a disadvantage, although the same traits are not necessarily disadvantageous in other contexts.

Change the Child or Change How He Is Taught?

If the learning of poor children is to be improved by treating their deficits, a very far-reaching treatment is likely to be required. It will not be enough simply to provide educationally enriching experience, as Head Start has tried to do with such disappointing results. Neither will it suffice to teach children Standard English or to provide intellectual experience with a view to developing their mental abilities. It will probably be necessary to do something to increase achievement motivation, to tone down children's levels of physical activity, to make them better able to concentrate and give thought to school tasks. Their interests may need to be conditioned so that they are more compatible with school subject matter. In short, poor children will need more-or-less to be made over from top to bottom, and this will probably require rather powerful intervention into their lives from an early age, with continued intervention throughout childhood to offset the effects of their environments and/or natural tendencies.

It is a big job and one that ought to give any educator serious qualms. The changes, if they are effective, will necessarily have effects that reach far beyond school learning. They would amount in essence to destruction of one life style and culture and its replacement by another. Even if one thinks such replacement would be a good thing (and I don't see how anyone could consider it an unmixed blessing), it is arrogant in the extreme to impose such a change merely in the interests of better school achievement.

An intelligent advocate of the difference approach cannot get by with denying that poor children have deficits with respect to school learning as it is now carried out. The challenge he must face is to discover new ways for poor children to learn that will not depend on traits in which the children are deficient. For instance, poor children tend to be what is called hyperactive. In plainer words, they tend to be excitable, impulsive, and disinclined to sit still for the long periods of time that school learning typically requires. Accordingly, one might look for an approach to learning that allowed children to be physically active. This is an appealing notion, but a difficult one to realize. Can reading, for instance, be learned by someone who is in a state of high arousal and activity? May it not be an intrinsic characteristic of the reading process itself that it requires a relaxed, sedentary kind of concentration? And can a person learn to read if he is not interested in anything that is not of immediate practical or sensual value? Perhaps. It remains to be seen.[5]

What of IQ and specific relevant intellectual abilities? Can reading be presented in such a way that it is learnable by children who are deficient in these? Perhaps the reason IQ is of so much concern

[5] As it happens, I myself am working now on an alternative method for teaching reading, that centers around body movement and social interaction. If it proves effective it should be a boon to the many children who have trouble sitting still to learn, but it is far too early to predict how it will turn out.

is that it appears to be a *sine qua non* of successful learning, as if no matter how learning is carried out you still have to have an average degree of intelligence to succeed at it. Actually, as I shall point out later, there is reason to believe that intelligence is not the inescapable necessity it is assumed to be. On the other hand, most innovations in teaching, such as the informal methods now in vogue, put more rather than less demands on intelligence than the conventional methods. Thus a "difference" approach that really tried to come to grips with reality would have to devise means of learning that required less of the kinds of intellectual abilities tapped by IQ tests.

The difference advocates have not shown much willingness to come to grips with reality. Instead they have tried romantically to distort reality so as to make their job look easy: relieve kids of the pressure to perform, treat them with respect, let them act out their impulses, let nature take its course, and they will learn. The result, in the more successful cases, has been schools in which poor kids are happier, and that is certainly something, but it hasn't solved the problem of their failure to acquire the basic skills of literacy and number and to acquire the kinds of knowledge that would equip them to do what they want with their lives.

Radical innovations that truly changed the conditions of learning so that they conformed to the characteristics of disadvantaged children might work but they would be risky. For instance, one approach to reading that might work would be to delay teaching it until the children had already acquired a firm sense of its value and until they had matured enough that they were more amenable to the work involved. That might mean waiting until they were in their teens or near to it. This has proved to be too radical a departure from custom even for most free school enthusiasts, although they often voice approval of the idea. Radical departures of this kind are risky in much the same way as the radical interventions of the "deficit" theorists are risky: they are bound to have side-effects that penetrate into other areas of the children's lives and there is no telling what all these effects might be. Such radical interventions are unavoidably separatist in their effect. They imply markedly different educations for different subcultural groups so that children from these different groups would enter adulthood with developmental histories that are even more different than they are now. This could have drastic social consequences that might be good or might be bad, but regardless of how an educator feels about the prospects, he ought to have qualms about taking such a role in other people's fates. Such radical changes are also separatist in the sense that they impose differences on whole groups of people when they may not be good for many individuals within these groups. By no means are all lower-class children deficient in aptitude for conventional school learning, and to force them into separate streams because of their ethnic identity would be a grave sort of discrimination.

Skills for All

The essential things that people need help in learning are few in number. At a minimum they consist of reading, writing, and practical uses of arithmetic. Above the minimum we might add the ability to reason logically and critically, although what people acquire of such ability now probably owes very little to teaching. We could go on to indicate a variety of kinds of knowledge that is generally valuable, but the domains are so broad and the efforts to teach them so unsuccessful with most people that it would be presumptuous to set them down as essential. We are left then with the three R's. They are what we expect kids to get out of school now, and these modest expectations are largely unmet in the case of poor children. If we could succeed in teaching them, we would have dealt with the main problem of inequality in learning among socioeconomic groups.

These basic skills, I maintain, can be taught to virtually everyone. They can be taught in ways that don't require as much intellectual ability and concentrated effort as present methods require. In experiments that I have had a part in, working with disadvantaged children, we have been able to teach them all to read and write by the time they were six years old.[6] We have also made considerable progress in teaching them arithmetic by that age, although I think there is more work to be done in that area, and I am presently involved in it. I don't say that all children should be taught these

[6] See especially the reports in vol. 2 of *Research and Development Program on Preschool Disadvantaged Children,* ed. Merle B. Karnes (Final Report of OE Project No. 5–1181, U.S. Office of Education, 1969).

skills by the age of six or that it can be done under normal teaching conditions, but it does seem that most of the job can be accomplished by the age of nine and I don't see any particular reason why it should not be.

What is required? Mainly, a well-organized program of instruction that makes learning easy by leaving as little as possible to the cleverness and determination of the child. You don't expect a child to discover for himself how letters spell words, you teach him how to figure out what a word spells. You don't expect a child to understand the foundations of arithmetic, you teach him how to think numerically. He may or may not think cleverly but he thinks soundly. It addition to good programs you need teachers who are willing to act as trainers, to follow the programs, to concentrate on mastery rather than on providing experiences or stimulating personal growth, and to make learning fun and rewarding for children regardless of their dispositions. Most school teaching is so disorganized, has so many gaps in it, that it places excessive demands on the less talented children and generates learning disabilities right and left among children who for any reason aren't in top shape for the game.

Even in the best of training programs, scholastic aptitude—the constellation of mental and personality traits we have discussed previously—will be an asset. Those with more aptitude will learn faster and go farther. The point is that high scholastic aptitude should not have to be a requirement for eventual mastery. It shouldn't be necessary to embark on drastic interventions to produce scholastic aptitude in order for children to acquire the essential skills.

Learning to swim provides an instructive analogy. In learning to swim it is a distinct asset to be relatively fearless in water and to have good physical coordination. Thus these characteristics are a part of aptitude for swimming, just as high IQ and visual memory are part of aptitude for reading. One approach to teaching swimming would be to start when children are little and spend years cultivating fearlessness and physical coordination. It might be beneficial, but it also might have undesirable side effects. Moreover it would involve substantial intervention into the normal childhood experience of many children; it would involve in some degree making children over into other kinds of children; and it would probably also require compulsion and hence infringement on individual liberties, since many parents and children would not go for it voluntarily. But this method isn't necessary. Swimming can be taught to children who are uncoordinated and afraid of the water—by some methods, though not by others.

No doubt this analogy occurs to me because I myself was a child who was afraid of the water and not very good at getting my arms and legs to do the required things coordinately. Thus I was a disadvantaged child as far as aptitude for swimming was concerned. In fact, I didn't learn to swim even after years of informal learning experience at the beach and bungling instruction that made no attempt at teaching one to relax in the water or at teaching swimming skills in a way that made them easy to coordinate. Finally I learned, quickly and rather well, in a university course with an instructor who knew how to teach. Training in swimming is much better now than it was thirty years ago. It doesn't take much aptitude to learn anymore. The same cannot be said of training in the three R's.

I am proposing something that has features of both the "deficit" and the "difference" approach. It recognizes deficiencies in children that have to be overcome, but it doesn't propose remaking children to remove the deficiencies. It proposes teaching in ways that minimize the effect of those deficiencies, or that at any rate make them no longer critical. Like the "difference" approach, it proposes changing teaching to suit the child, but it is basically universalist rather than separatist in its thrust. It proposes giving everyone a minimum set of skills by essentially the same means.

Such training in basic skills will not achieve equality. Opportunities for extended learning beyond the minimum should be available to all, but we should recognize that they will not be exploited equally by all. I do not see any way around that fact, short of making everybody over into some lowest common denominator.

In a system that was truly dedicated to turning educational choices over to parents and children, there should be options available for radical reshaping of children. Some lower-class people might really want to be made over so as to have the characteristics associated with scholastic aptitude. To deny such an option would be almost as high-handed as to force it upon all poor people. What is likely to be most in demand however, by rich and poor alike, is solid training in basic skills without a lot of educational frills attached. In a free market for training services, there is no doubt that poor people would be more liable to get stuck with bad buys in training, just as they now get stuck with bad buys in food and medicine. Consumer protection can do something to minimize these misfortunes, but they can't be eliminated without a dictatorship that makes people's choices for them. That is what we have now in education, and it does not appear to be serving the poor very well.

The answer to the question raised in the title of this chapter is, by all indications, *yes.* Inequality is here to stay. But there can be less of it, it can be fairer, and—perhaps most importantly—the minimum levels of attainment can be raised. School and teaching have a very limited role to play. They can do little to eliminate inequality, but they can do something to raise the minimum level of the skills people have for making their way in the world.

chapter five

The Institutionalization of Personal Choice

In previous chapters I have argued that public institutions shouldn't set goals for people, shouldn't try to influence what kind of adults children turn out to be, shouldn't decide that a group of people ought to be assimilated into the mainstream culture or separated from it. In short, the government ought to leave people alone. This seems to add up to anarchism of the peaceful type so appealingly advocated by Paul Goodman.[1]

On the other hand I have suggested a number of things that ought to be provided at public expense, and I will suggest a number more in later chapters of this book—all sorts of training, counseling, community centers, child care, ultimately even education. All of this bespeaks big government, with even more involvement in the lives of people than government has now.

How are these positions to be reconciled? To answer this question we must look beyond education and consider at a basic level the role of public institutions in private and communal life. Such a consideration is the starting point of Ivan Illich's critique of schooling, and so we would do well to look first at his analysis.

To Illich, as I understand him, the inherent evil of schooling is that the process of going to school replaces personal competence as a value—just as going to a doctor replaces health, and law en-

[1] See, for instance, Paul Goodman, *Utopian Essays and Practical Proposals* (New York: Vintage Books, 1964).

forcement replaces moral conduct. This replacement he calls the "institutionalization of values."[2] People become dependent on institutions to determine their values and these institutionalized values become ones that can be realized only through the institutions. In the end, he says, "all our activities tend to take the shape of client relationships to other specialized institutions."[3]

Institutionalization has its strongest impact on the poor, because of their social powerlessness. Illich speaks of "modernized poverty" in which the poor are not merely exploited by landlords and merchants but are subjugated in every aspect of their lives by institutions created to help them.

> *For instance, the U.S. poor can count on a truant officer to return their children to school . . . or on a doctor to assign them to a hospital bed which costs sixty dollars a day . . . But such care only makes them dependent on more treatment, and renders them increasingly incapable of organizing their own lives around their own experiences and resources within their own communities.*[4]

Schools, says Illich, not only make people dependent on schooling, but they condition people to be dependent on institutionalized values in all other aspects of their lives. Instead of self-reliant individuals they become insatiable consumers of services and products, their need for which is generated by the same institutions that supply the services and products. The image that comes to mind is that of commercially produced hogs, spending their lives at the feeding trough consuming the contrived diets provided for them, their appetites stimulated and their tendencies toward physical activity suppressed by drugs and hormones incorporated into the very food they eat.

The trend toward this dehumanized condition must be reversed, and Illich sees deschooling as the place to start. Schools he classifies along with prisons, hospitals, superhighways, and most consumer good industries, as *manipulative* institutions. Manipulative institutions produce dependency by generating the need for their "products" and by controlling in one way or other the way their products are used. Schools, prisons, and hospitals turn out people

[2] Ivan Illich, *Deschooling Society* (New York: Harrow Books, 1972).
[3] *Ibid.*, p. 56.
[4] *Ibid.*, p. 6.

who need more schooling, imprisonment, or hospitalization and, once conditioned to this need, people can obtain learning, rehabilitation, or health only in ways prescribed by the institutions. Manufacturers create the need through advertising and the products are designed in the manner of washing machines that determine how one does one's laundry and generate additional dependencies on certain kinds of soap, repair services, housing arrangements, and so on.

Contrasted with manipulative institutions are what Illich calls convivial institutions and what his colleague, Reimer, calls democratic institutions. These are institutions that satisfy a need without creating a dependency; they are there when you need them without generating increasing needs. They can serve a diversity of individual purposes, thus increasing rather than controlling the options available to people. The best examples are public utilities, such as electricity. According to Reimer they take the form of networks rather than production systems.[5]

Illich's scheme for learning nets as an alternative to schools represents an attempt to design a convivial or democratic institution to replace a manipulative one. The learning nets are computer networks whereby people can locate things and other people for their individual learning needs.

A common device for ignoring criticism is to pressure the critic into proposing an alternative to the thing he is criticizing and then direct attention to finding fault with his proposal. This has unfortunately happened with Illich. His penetrating criticism of modern institutions has tended to be ignored by educators, who concentrate on predicting dire consequences of deschooling.[6] I am not very enthusiastic about the learning net idea. I don't think many people would bother to use the facility. But I think Illich's analysis of institutional dependency is profound and should not be ignored by anyone who is concerned with the future of individual integrity in the modern world.

[5] Reimer, *School Is Dead.*

[6] D. U. Levine and R. J. Havighurst, eds., *Farewell to Schools???* (Belmont, Calif.: Wadsworth, 1971).

An Alternative to Deinstitutionalization

The problem that Illich has raised can be restated as follows: modern institutions are progressively gaining control over individual decision making. Galbraith has made the same point about giant industries.[7] When they undertake to produce a new product their investment is so great that they are unwilling to take a chance on the whims of individual taste. Thus upwards of half the cost of a product may be in getting the consumer to buy it—a cost that is borne, of course, by the consumer himself. Public institutions don't operate in quite the same way (although the Pentagon has an enormous public relations and propaganda budget, aimed at increasing public acceptance of its not-very-palatable product). They guarantee a market by other, even more insidious means than sales pitches, such as the following:

1. Monopoly

The convict and the welfare recipient have no choice of services. They must take what others have decided is best for them. If he has money, the learner has a choice between public and private schools, but all come ultimately under control of the state. Without money, the learner must go to the state's schools.

2. Compulsion

Besides the obvious examples of compulsory schooling and imprisonment there are compulsory treatment for alleged mental illness and compulsory embalming of corpses that are destined to be cremated—surely the most grotesque instance of compulsory institutional dependency around.

[7] John Kenneth Galbraith, *The New Industrial State* (Boston: Houghton Mifflin Co., 1967).

3. CREDENTIALING

This is just a shade short of compulsion. No one says you have to be a doctor or a teacher, but if you want to become one then you have to submit yourself to a prescribed course of institutional processing. The most rampant form of credentialing, however, is of a less official sort. The world is full of jobs that require no particular prior learning, and yet you stand little chance of being hired for them unless you have a high school diploma or a college degree, depending on the status of the job.

4. BENEFITS WITH STRINGS ATTACHED

Government health insurance allows a choice of practitioners, but only those who are acceptable to the medical establishment. The GI bill and the current experiment with educational vouchers allow learners a choice only among recognized establishments. When a person accepts welfare payments he falls under a variety of requirements as to how the money may be spent, who may live in the household, and so on. And the recipient must often agree to undergo prescribed training or treatment as a "case." Welfare services, indeed, constitute a kind of second educational system in which participation is virtually as compulsory as it is in the first.

To these we should add advertising, which is coming more and more to be used where other devices fail in generating dependency on educational institutions. The school dropout cannot ride a bus without encountering an ad designed to frighten or humiliate him into going back to school. Educational associations sponsor billboards and TV spot announcements to promote greater expenditures on schools.

Short of revolution, it seems to me that the way to attack the encroachment of institutions on individual decision-making is by regulating the means by which needs are controlled. In the private sector it would make sense to regulate the amount that industries could spend on sales and promotion and still claim as a business expense. If over a quarter of the cost of a product or service goes into selling it, then it seems obvious the public is being sold something it doesn't really want. If the project is a necessity, then the consumer is being subjected to extortion in having to pay so much to be sold something that he would buy anyway. It would be interesting to see a law suit in which the plaintiff objected to paying the full price of a new automobile on grounds that he had not exposed himself to any advertising but had merely read *Consumer Reports* and gone to the dealer and told him what he wanted.

In dealing with public institutions the attack on management of need would have to be much more complex, and would vary from institution to institution. For that reason I will deal only with schools, although other institutions such as welfare and law enforcement provide interesting subjects for speculation. With schools the obvious starting point is the elimination of compulsory attendance. We have already discussed this matter in the preceding chapter in the context of individual liberties. From the standpoint of decreasing dependency on schools as controllers of individual decisions, the elimination of compulsory attendance would not be much of an accomplishment since, if nothing else changed, most people would still be as dependent as they are now.

The more important target is credentialing. If it were made unlawful for employers or professions to require schooling, if they could only require evidence of competence, the whole burden of decision-making would shift back towards the indivdual. A government employment agency could provide a service for testing and certifying various competencies, but such a service would have the character of a democratic institution in Reimer's terms. It would be there for whoever needed it, but it would not control the processes by which competence was achieved.

Finally, there should be an end to educational monopoly. A system of learning vouchers with minimum strings attached would allow an open market in services to learners. The state could provide learning resources—training programs and the like—but private services should be able to compete fairly with them. To keep out swindlers and charlatans, the preferred method would not be licensing, which would invite state control, but requirements of full disclosure and truth in advertising.

By such changes, considerable institutional reform would probably take place as a natural consequence. Educational concerns would have to become more responsive to people's needs and they would be dispossessed of their power to impose their own ideas of what is good for people. Basic value choices and the responsibility for direction of their lives would in a considerable measure, at least, return to the people.

The Public Interest

Unfortunately, governments cannot help but act to some extent as educators. Government actions influence how people develop, whether the influences are intentional or not. According to Cyril Burt's data on the scholastic attainment of London school children, covering more than half a century, the most significant influences on children's learning were the two World Wars.[8] Achievement and intelligence test scores dropped markedly during and for a time after each war. Responsible officials will pay attention to such effects. Given a choice they will prefer government actions that, in their judgment, will have a good effect on people to ones that will have a bad effect. Hence they will function as educators.

There are several kinds of government action that deserve special attention from an educational point of view. The most important kind includes all government actions that attempt to change individual behavior for public good. A great deal of this is seen in wartime—rationing, censorship, patriotic propaganda, and the like. A current example is the effort in some countries to control population growth by inducing individual citizens to have fewer children. This effort is commonly spoken of as an educational effort, although its primary purpose obviously is not to improve people but to limit population.

In attempting to protect the public from harm, governments often engage in what may be called "negative education." The term comes from Rousseau, who held that this was the most important kind of education for children up to the age of twelve: "It consists not in teaching virtue and truth, but in preserving the heart from vice and the mind from error." Censorship comes immediately to mind, but blue laws in general are a form of negative education, preventing people from having certain experiences that might influ-

[8] Cyril Burt, "Recent Studies of Abilities," *Journal of the Association of Educational Psychologists* 2 (1969).

ence their development in ways judged as bad by the lawmakers. More generally, all government actions aimed at protecting us from harm—be it the policeman at the crosswalk or the fire inspector checking wiring—also prevent us from learning what might be learned from our own mistakes or misfortune.

Governments also educate through public works. When a government erects a monument, embarks on redevelopment of an urban area, establishes a museum, or creates a public beach, it necessarily imposes esthetic and social values on people. Even if public works are decided upon in a democratic way, which they seldom are, the prevailing values are imposed on dissenting minorities as well.

Finally, governments cannot help but exert educational influence simply because they must decide what services to provide out of limited resources. If anyone who wanted to could start a television station, there would be no need for government involvement. But, because channels are limited, we have licensing of TV stations with the result that government officials are put into the position of deciding what is good for us in the way of television viewing. If it were possible to provide at public expense every possible sort of educational experience for children, and the users had free choice, then one could speak of a public education system that did not impose values on people. Given limited resources, choices have to be made above the level of the individual. The individual is at least limited to a choice among the most popular alternatives.

These forms of imposition, if one may use so harsh a word, are inevitable if a government is to act in the public interest. Governments that are sensitive to individual wants will try to plan things that minimize imposition. They will prefer general-purpose parks to centers of organized recreation. But they will recognize that these, too, impose value choices; and so they will also provide organized recreational facilities because, for instance, you can't play handball or fire pottery in an open field and some people, who can't afford their own facilities, like to do such things. With limited resources it may come down to providing either a handball court or a pottery kiln, but not both, and so someone is going to have to decide which need is more worthy of being met.

It is tempting to give up at this point and say, "If the government is going to act as educator no matter what, then we might as well make the most of it and have a public educational system that gives everyone the best education possible under the circumstances." In other words, keep the present system while trying, as always, to improve it.

Two important arguments can be made against this laissez-faire attitude. The first is that there is a difference between, on one hand, the inevitable educational effect of governmental actions taken in the public interest and, on the other hand, the establishment of institutions whose main function is to replace individual initiative with public policy. There is a difference, in other words, between law enforcement, which we must have in some form, and educating people to become law-abiding citizens. There is a difference between providing historical museums and teaching history, even though both may be biased. And there is a difference between supplementing the incomes of poor people and providing social workers to "improve" the way poor people live and spend their money. The difference may be only one of degree, but it is a large difference when measured by the extent to which values are imposed and life decisions are taken out of people's hands.

The other argument is that, even though governmental actions necessarily have an educational effect, there can be a great difference in effect depending on the attitude officials have toward their power to educate. Governments must engage in social planning, regulation, public works, and services. The planners, lawmakers, and bureaucrats involved in such activities are human beings with ample opportunities to abuse their powers. Checks on abuses can only go so far; in the end a great deal depends on the good intentions of the people involved, and here it makes a difference what is considered an abuse and what isn't.

The official who sees construction of a museum largely as an opportunity to make money for his brother-in-law's construction company is clearly recognized as abusing his power. The official who sees construction of a museum as an opportunity to impose his esthetic or patriotic ideals on the masses is more likely to be seen as a statesman. It is this view—a very ancient one, to be sure, dating at least from the great age of Athens—that needs to be brought under criticism.

I would hold that the public employee—be he lawmaker, administrator, or teacher—who uses his position to educate, who performs his job with the ulterior motive of improving people and getting them to behave according to different values, is abusing his power. Such abuse is exceedingly widespread, but in large part, I think, because it is condoned without question. My main purpose in writing this book is to get people to question educational motives.

PART II

ALTERNATIVES TO EDUCATION

chapter six

Schools Without Education*

Regardless of what happens to education, something like the elementary school is bound to continue to exist—not because it performs a vital function but because it is a convenience. There is a need for children to be taken care of during the day outside their homes. The local school is a convenient setting for such care. It can house many cultural resources and serve as a departure point for others out in the community. It can also house some of the more common kinds of training that will be needed for most children, such as training in the three R's. It could be just a place, with different people doing different things in it. It would not need to have any unifying purpose, least of all the purpose of educating children.

What I propose that schools should be is essentially what they are now, only better. For there is no evidence that schools accomplish anything beyond training and child care. Education amounts to an empty claim, but in trying to make good on the claim, schools waste money and energy, subject children to endless tedium, and end up doing an inferior job of what they do do.

What we find in the elementary schools now is an idealistic commitment to the *idea* of education on the part of people who

* "Schools Without Education," appeared in an expanded form in the *Harvard Educational Review* 42 (1972): 390–413.

were mainly drawn into teaching because of a liking for children —whose actual motivations, in other words, are toward child care. The weight of opinion from all sources compels teachers to think of themselves as educators, for wherever they turn child care is spoken of condescendingly and training is usually spoken of with contempt. Yet at the same time the schools are under daily attack for doing a bad job, and it is not for failing to educate but for doing a poor job of child care and training.

School as a Place to Be

"Most schools," says John Holt, "remain about what they have always been, bad places for children, or, for that matter, anyone to be in, to live in, to learn in." [1] What goes on there, we are told by numerous observers, is nonsensical and degrading. Children are bored and humiliated. Schools are continually likened to prisons.

Holt intimates that schools have always been that way and we are just beginning to notice. Defenders point out that the great majority of children claim to like school. Both, it seems to me, overlook what is a fairly clear historical record showing that school as a place to be has changed a good deal in recent centuries and is now changing again.

Phillipe Ariés has traced the evolution of schools from the medieval colleges, which were rather like open universities, to custodial institutions where children of a certain age were kept.[2] Harsh discipline enforced upon surly and rebellious children became the rule. In sixteenth-century England, it is reported, flogging demonstrations were part of the graduation exercises for prospective Latin masters.[3] In 1790 Benjamin Rush observed that the spread of more humane and civilized ways of treating people had not yet reached the schools: "The rod is yet the principal instrument of governing them, and a school-master remains the only despot known in free

[1] John Holt, *The Underachieving School* (New York: Delta Books, 1969), pp. 15–16.

[2] Phillipe Ariés, *Centuries of Childhood* (New York: Random House, 1962).

[3] P. R. Cole, *A History of Educational Thought* (London: Oxford University Press, 1931), p. 160.

countries."[4] Although changes took place earlier in some other countries, it could be said that down to the middle of the nineteenth century a state of martial law characterized the schools of England, Canada, and the United States.[5]

By no reasonable standard could such schools be considered good places for children to be. They were disorderly, stressful, and often unstable. An amazing transformation then occurred in which schools became not only tolerable but valued and integral parts of the lives of most children. I speak now of the kinds of elementary schools attended by most adults now living.

The kind of school that emerged in the latter half of the nineteenth century is the kind that we now call "traditional" and which is the object of so much ridicule. It would pay us, however, to look at some of its good features, for it had more to be said for it than merely the absence of brutal treatment of children. Firstly, the traditional school was—in contrast to earlier schools and some urban schools today—a safe and peaceful place for children to be. We tend to regard peace and safety as normal and therefore don't seek to account for them, but it would appear that in school they are not to be taken for granted and are not achieved without some effort and design. A second fact to note about life in the traditional school is that most children expressed satisfaction with it—about 80 percent, according to various studies conducted over a span of forty years.[6]

There is a more significant virtue of traditional school life, however, which I do not know how to document and which I must therefore ask the reader to check against his own experience and observations. It is that in the traditional school children generally felt that what they were doing was important. If true, this is no small credit to school as a place for children to be; for in the modern world at large what children do is not important. They have no economic value except as modest consumers; they have no po-

[4] From an extract in E. W. Knight and C. L. Hall, eds., *Readings in American Educational History* (New York: Greenwood Press, 1951), p. 473

[5] Paul Munroe, "History of Corporal Punishment," in *Cyclopedia of Education,* vol. 5 (New York: Macmillan Co., 1913); F. H. Johnson, "Changing Conceptions of Discipline and Pupil-Teacher Relations in Canadian Schools" (Doctoral dissertation, University of Toronto, 1952).

[6] P. W. Jackson, *Life in Classrooms* (New York: Holt, Rinehart, and Winston, 1968), pp. 41–81.

litical force, are incapable of any impact on the course of events; with rare exceptions they do not say or do anything that is of interest to anyone except those who dote on them. Paul Goodman has criticized schools for maintaining young people in a state of uselessness, cut off from the significant work of the world. Goodman was talking about adolescents, and with respect to them the criticism has force. But with respect to children an opposite case can be made—that in a world that has little call for their services, the school provides children with an artificial environment where they are needed and where their efforts count for something.

I mention these three virtues of traditional school life—peace, enjoyment, and the child's sense that what he does is important—because they are qualities one would seek in any kind of child-care facility and because they are qualities that present-day critics find lacking in schools. Indeed, much of the concern in alternative schools, such as the First Street School described by George Dennison,[7] is to regain these elemental qualities.

How were they achieved in the traditional school? I would suggest three familiar features of the traditional school that fairly well epitomize its way of functioning. They are *working for marks, ritual,* and *"good student" morality.*

WORKING FOR MARKS

Work, though seldom arduous, occupied much of the time in a traditional school—lessons, recitations, "seat" work, homework, "projects," and the like. The theoretical outcome of all this work was learning, but from the immediate standpoint of both teacher and child, the outcome was marks. The mutual involvement of teacher and child in working for marks is important to note. The teacher did not merely dispense the marks and other evaluations of the child's work but also devoted herself to helping the child improve those marks. Good marks, symbolizing the doing of good work, constituted a shared goal that gave coherence and direction to what would otherwise be rather pointless efforts on the part of pupils and teachers.

[7] George Dennison, *The Lives of Children* (New York: Random House, 1969).

Ritual

From opening exercises to procedures for donning coats and boots at the close of the day, traditional school life was highly ritualized. For virtually everything that was done in school there was a certain way to do it, and traditional school life was in part a continued painstaking struggle to do everything the way it was supposed to be done. Some things were difficult to master, like the requirements for a presentable piece of written work. Others, like the rituals of oral recitation, were so easily learned that many young children knew how to act them out before they had even entered school, having learned them by playing school with older children.

"Good student" morality

In contrast to the vagueness with which good citizenship is defined in the world at large, there was no question in the traditional school as to what good citizenship entailed. It meant, primarily, doing one's best at all times in the collective effort to do good work and to observe the rituals. The rituals and the work assignments specified the behaviors that constituted being a good student; all that remained for the child was to supply the effort and hopefully a certain amount of aptitude for the job.

These three features of traditional school life—working for marks, ritual, and "good student" morality—are the very characteristics most thoroughly damned by modern critics, for whom they spell joyless drudgery, artificiality, meaninglessness, and destruction of individuality. On the other hand, it is these same characteristics that seem best able to account for the good qualities of traditional school life.

Ritual, clear-cut morality, and a definite job to do obviously contribute to a peaceful and orderly school life. If they are not exactly a prescription for pleasure they are at least a defense against aimless boredom. But most especially they provide the foundation for a way of life in which children feel what they do is important. Consider the child's school work. Pointless as it might be from a detached adult perspective, irrelevant as much of it was to any worthwhile learning, within the school context the child's work really mattered. To his teacher it mattered whether the work was done on time and done right. Her seriousness on this account, expressed through report card grades, caused the child's work to matter to his parents as well. Thus, artificial as it might be, the child had a job that was more meaningful than many a job in the real world, for it involved a striving for excellence that the more routine jobs lack. Ritual also bestows importance upon the individual's actions, as shown for instance by the significance that the acts of sitting and standing have in a church service compared with the significance they have in an informal social gathering. Viewed from outside, ritual is absurd, but to the involved participant (and I am sure that many of today's critics were once involved participants in the school rituals) rituals mean something.

The situation in a traditional school has much similarity to the situation in a peacetime army. Both the child and the peacetime soldier are being readied for future activity, but in both cases the future activity is too remote and unforeseeable to serve as adequate motivation or purpose on a day-to-day basis. There being no real accomplishments to strive for, an artificial world is generated in which work of no actual consequence becomes invested with importance by being used as a running test of merit. All aspects of life become highly ritualized and so much emotion becomes attached to the rituals that even minor deviations from them are seen as threatening to the whole structure of life. The guiding purpose in life becomes not that of achieving any external objective but that of being a good pupil or a good soldier as the case may be.

"Morale" is the military term referring to how well this artificial system functions. It appears the system never works too well in the peacetime military. Adults are simply too sophisticated to accept the necessary assumptions. Schools, dealing with a more naive membership, have enjoyed much greater success, but that seems to be changing. The declining faith of educators in the traditional school way of life can be traced back for decades—an increasing diffidence about assigning grades, a shift of concern from the quality of a child's work to a concern with his personal development, a deemphasis of ritual in favor of naturalness and informality, a gradual softening of the line on matters of neatness, etiquette, posture, and the like. More recently one may observe among school children a sophisticated detachment that is disastrous for the traditional school way of life. The word seems to have passed down from college to high school and now to the more with-it elementary school populations that a great deal of school work is pointless, that grades don't really tell how good you are, and that the school rituals are a subject for derision.

What seems to be happening is that the perspective of the outer world is penetrating the school. The traditional school cannot survive such an invasion, for if goings on in school come to be judged by the same standards as goings-on outside they will be seen as ridiculous and the structure will collapse. You cannot have a room full of ten-year-old Paul Goodmans and Edgar Z. Friedenbergs and hope to run a traditional school, especially if the teacher holds the same viewpoint.

Some new mode of child care is going to have to emerge. There is plenty of room for it to be better than traditional schooling ever was. The trick will be to evolve some new condition, not based on ritual and contrived "work," which enables children to feel that they are spending their days on worthwhile and meaningful things.

preparing for life
good teaching in
the school

Informal Schooling as Child Care

The answer to the need for a new mode of child care for school age children may already be in front of us in the shape of the informal school. The informal school (which refers to roughly the same thing as the open concept and the English infant school model) is represented as a new approach to education rather than to child care. But as an approach to education it is difficult to see what there is to get excited about. Informal schooling has not demonstrated any remarkable achievements of an educational sort; the main ideas are the familiar ones of progressive education; and the kinds of learning activities that go on are, for the most part, ones that can be observed in traditional schools as well. What seems to impress people about informal schools, what brings them back oohing and aahing from England, is the style of life in the schools.

Children in the informal schools, we are told, seem so secure; they are so happy and so involved in what they are doing. All this sounds very familiar, but there does indeed seem to be a difference between life in a well-functioning informal school and life in a well-functioning traditional school. Mainly, I would say, it is that the children seem more natural. They move around, talk to each other, and poke into things more like the way they do in their out-of-school life. One is struck by the lack of ritualized speech and action and by the lack of striving to perform.

How does the informal school manage to function without benefit of ritual and working for grades? I hope I may be excused for not quoting explanations given by the leading thinkers associated with informal education: I find their theorizing to be unbearably maudlin. The simple fact, which does not really demand much explanation, seems to be this: *given an ample choice of activities deemed worthwhile and some help in making up their minds, children will tend to engage themselves in worthwhile activities.*

Now if that is all there is to it, one may wonder why it took school people five hundred years, most of which were spent whacking children with sticks, before the truth dawned on them. The answer, I think, is not that people were blind or were stuck on the idea of original sin. I think people have probably always recognized the above principle as a sensible guide to child tending, but only recently has it occurred to them to call it education.

Although in practice a good deal of educational effort goes on in informal schools, the underlying idea of informal schooling is non-educational. It is to provide a suitable environment for children to live and grow in. The child's life and destiny are essentially his own, with the teacher as an adjunct to nature rather than an agent of society charged with making the child turn out the way society wishes. This is a philosophy of child care, and a rather good one. Its full application is hampered, however, by the unfortunate belief that it is a philosophy of education.

A well-functioning informal school provides excellent child care: a safe, pleasant place for children to be with each other, with many more interesting things to do than are available at home, and some helpful adults around in case they are needed. The effects of adding educational effort to this child care are minor but, I think, wholly negative. In the name of education there is less freedom of choice than there would otherwise be. For some activities all the child is actually free to choose is when he will do them, not whether; and these tend to be the duller and more pointless activities such as social science projects, which, in informal schools as in traditional ones, amount to cutting pictures out of magazines and copying passages out of encyclopedias. Educational purpose dictates a certain concern about "progress," which may take the form of evaluations, conferences, progress charts, etc. It is also likely that the range of activities made available to children is narrowed somewhat by the need to give a justification, however flimsy, for each activity in terms of its educational value. Finally, educational purpose keeps teachers involved in a lot of effort to observe, understand, anticipate, and respond to everything that is going on with each child, even though the calculated effect of their effort, both in fact and in principle, is nil: it is all like straining to help the bus get there faster.

Perhaps there are more sinister implications to education carried out in informal schools. Lillian Weber quotes with approval a publication of England's National Froebel Foundation that claims teachers in informal schools actually have a "more active directing part to play" than teachers in traditional schools. The statement goes on to explain:

> *But the part to be played is of course a very different kind. It is based on not imposing anything on children, but on so closely cooperating with their native interests and drives that whatever they are led to do is felt as something that comes out of themselves.*[8]

Shades of Walden Two! The statement implies a kind of education against which children would have no defense, since they would not know when they were being influenced.

Any kind of child care will, of course, tend to mold children in some nonrandom way. Since children cannot be wholly the architects of their own environments, their environments will inevitably reflect some particular adults' notions as to what is suitable for them. Furthermore, as anyone who has worked with young children knows, some of them demand help in deciding what to do with their time and others become bored and troublesome if they don't get it, so that adults unavoidably bias children's choices of activities. That much we can accept as a fact of life in any institutionalized form of child care. But it is one thing for an adult to recognize his

[8] Weber, *English Infant School,* p. 109.

tendency to bias the course of child development and try to minimize this effect and another thing for him to regard such biasing as his mission. The first is responsible child care; the second is education.

Separating Training from Child Care

Not only has the traditional school failed to satisfy one out of five of its pupils, it has also failed a large number of them in its responsibility to teach the basic skills of reading, writing, and arithmetic. Estimating what proportion of children it fails is a complex matter involving judgments not only as to what constitutes failure but also, as to how many children could have succeeded under more favorable conditions. But the proportion of failures may not need to be established anyway since, whether they number two hundred or two million per year, the problem is not that society is burdened with an excessive number of illiterates and people who can't figure their income tax but, rather, that any children who had the potential to acquire the basic skills and were not given the opportunity to do so have been cruelly cheated by the schools. Everett Reimer has suggested that parents of such children should be able to sue the schools for damages. Whether the proposal is realistic or not, it at least makes us look at skill training from the proper perspective, seeing it as a matter of individual right rather than a matter of efficiency of the school system.

We are told that informal schools do as well at teaching reading as traditional schools and only a shade less well at teaching arithmetic computation.[9] While these results are a comfort to those who are switching over to the informal mode, they indicate that informal schooling does not promise any advance toward a solution of what may be called the problem of the skill-deprived child. Indeed, to me these results are mainly surprising for what they suggest about the ineffectiveness of skill training in the traditional schools.

[9] C. E. Silberman, *Crisis in the Classroom* (New York: Random House, 1970). For some less optimistic findings, however, see Joel Weiss, "Openness and Student Outcomes" (Paper presented at American Educational Research Association, New Orleans, February, 1973).

In the discussion that follows I shall deal mainly with learning to read, since it is clearly the most vital of the three R's and the one about which there has been the most study. If we take as a premise that a given child should be able to learn to read if a majority of children like him learn to read, then we may conclude that virtually all children in school are capable of learning to read. There exist now reading programs which, when properly executed, achieve 100 percent success in teaching beginning reading to children for whom the "normal" expectation of success is decidedly lower.[10] My purpose in mentioning this, however, is not to press for a particular method of attack on the reading problem but only to suggest that the problem is not one that has to wait for the unravelling of deep scientific mysteries before it can be solved. The unsolved problem is not how to get children to learn reading but how to get schools to teach it.

Teaching a child to read is a matter of training, and schools of both the traditional and informal type are, I suggest, poor situations for the conduct of training. Training may be briefly defined as the teaching of performance. Two clear-cut kinds of training that come immediately to mind in connection with schools are training in team sports and the training of a school band. In comparison to the other teaching functions of schools, these two tend to be highly successful, even in small schools where there is not much room for selection of talent.

These extracurricular kinds of training illustrate some of the characteristic features of training as it is carried out in the world

[10] I refer to the two most systematic intensive phonics programs I know of. One grew out of the academic preschool program conducted by Siegfried Engelmann and me, where one hundred percent success was achieved in teaching disadvantaged children to read by the end of kindergarten. See S. Engelmann, "The Effectiveness of Direct Instruction on IQ Performance and Achievement in Reading and Arithmetic," in *Disadvantaged Child 3,* ed. J. Hellmuth (New York: Brunner Mazel, Inc., 1970), pp. 339–61. Since developed by Englemann and others into the DISTAR program, it has had strikingly good results in Project Follow Through. See W. C. Becker, "Aptitude and Achievement from the Point of View of the Teacher" (Paper presented at CTB/McGraw-Hill Conference on the Aptitude-Achievement Distinction, Carmel, Calif., February, 1973). The other is the Open Court reading program, which since 1969 has guaranteed results in its first-grade program, and three years later has not yet had to refund any money, even though the program has been used widely in a variety of schools and even though the users have been able to choose the tests for evaluating results. See news release, Open Court Publishing Company, LaSalle, Illinois, December 1, 1971.

at large. (1) It is not carried out for its own sake but as a means of access to a desired activity. (2) It is separated from the rest of life and has its own criteria, which are different from general criteria of self-development. Thus, motivation and success are highly specific to the skill in question. (3) The training is carried out by someone whose responsibility and concern are rather narrowly confined to the performance being learned.

Training, on these three counts, is the opposite of school learning as it is usually conceived—that is, as learning which is carried out for its own sake, closely integrated with the overall development of the child, and guided by a teacher whose responsibility and concern for the child are essentially unbounded.

The reasons why traditional schools and informal schools are inhospitable to training have this much in common: both, in their own ways, seek to develop an internally consistent and harmonious way of school life. Thus various elements of schooling tend to lose their distinctiveness and to become like each other in sometimes absurd ways. The traditional school would at first glance seem well-suited to training since children are continually called on to perform, and their performance is continually evaluated. Indeed, the traditional school is permeated with training, to such an extent that training is sometimes applied grotesquely where it does not belong: instead of learning history children learn to perform a rotely memorized set of statements about history. But then, just as meaningful learning becomes contaminated with performance learning, so does skill training get muddled up with the effort to promote understanding, creativity, and the like. A reading lesson and a science lesson thus come to have much the same ingredients—a mishmash of memorization, drill, procedure learning, inquiry, question-and-answer recitation, factual exposition, craft projects, and free-floating discussion. Finally, in the traditional school there is the tendency for everything to become ritualized and shaped into some kind of routine work. Thus the goal of training, which is some ultimate ability to perform, is dissolved into a concern with the day-by-day performance of lesson rituals and work assignments that have only a nominal relevance to the training goal.

In informal schools the drive for consistency creates severe problems of reconciling training with the otherwise informal and undemanding character of the school. Jonathon Kozol has recently made the strong claim that free schools fail mainly because teachers in them do not pursue seriously enough their responsibility to train children in what he calls "survival skills." [11] He himself admits to using straightforward phonics training when it is needed. Apparently many teachers in informal settings, however, find it difficult to switch over into the role of trainer, nor is it surprising that they should. Nonauthoritarian parents also find it difficult to give their children formal training, because of the incongruity of the trainer and child-care roles.

Good training and good child care have almost nothing in common. Training is authoritarian by its very nature. If you signed up for swimming lessons and the teacher told you to swim however you liked, you would want your money back. Good child care on the other hand allows maximum reasonable freedom. Training has definite goals and aims to reach them; child care flows along indefinitely like life itself. Training is highly focussed; child care takes account of the whole child. Training aims at successful performance; child care is not judgmental—the child doesn't succeed or fail at it.

With such differences it stands to reason that training and child care should be separated; different kinds of people should provide them, under different circumstances. The child should know when he is in one and when he is in the other. The result of this separation should be a purer and more wholesome kind of child care along with training that is more lively and successful.

To the advocates of informal education, such separation is anathema. One of the central ideas of progressive education embodied in informal schools is that the artificial chopping up of the curriculum into subjects and the separation of all these subjects from life should be ended. The "integrated day," according to Lillian Weber is the ideal toward which informal educators strive.[12] This ideal is perfectly sound in those cases where training is not necessary. The farm boy lives an integrated day and in the process learns to ride a horse; the street child in a poor nation leads an integrated day hustling a living and in the process learns arithmetic; the immigrant child leads an integrated day and in the process learns a second language. But lacking these opportunities, other

[11] Jonathon Kozol, *Free Schools* (New York: Houghton Mifflin Co., 1972).
[12] Weber, *English Infant School*, p. 91.

children will not learn riding, arithmetic, or a second language unless they have specific training.

The need for training arises from the incompleteness of normal experience. To try to reshape the ordinary experience of children so that it includes all that is necessary for the natural acquisition of reading and numerical skills is to produce an absurdly artificial environment. (You see some of this in informal schools that go to ridiculous lengths to get children to count and measure everything that comes into view.) The more sensible approach would be to provide training with a minimum of fuss and wasted effort, and then simply provide enough resources in the environment for the child to put the skills to use if he feels inclined.

Practical Consideration

Take an ordinary old elementary school. Announce to the teachers that they can have their choice between being child care workers and scholastic skill trainers. Put the child care workers on the ground floor and tell them that their job is not to educate children but simply to provide them with an abundance of things to do in and out of school that will make for a good life. Put the trainers upstairs or in the basement, assign them either language arts or arithmetic as their subject, and tell them to find a way to teach it successfully to any child who walks in the door, using no more than three hours of his time per week. Give the child care workers an ample equipment and field-trip budget and give the trainers some time off to be trained themselves in any teaching method of their choice.

I believe this method of implementation, though far from ideal, would be a substantial improvement over most elementary school situations now. Probably more teachers would opt for child care than for training, and that would be all right, for it would probably work out that at any given time only a fourth to a third of the children would be in a training session. The child-care types, one might predict, would be relieved at having training responsibilities taken out of their hands and would develop an appealing collection of resources and activities. The training types, I suspect, would find the chance to specialize refreshing and would acquire striking proficiency at teaching their skills. Scheduling children's time for training so that it did not get too much in the way of other activities would be a headache, but it would be resolved somehow and children would find both kinds of school experience enjoyable in their different ways. In the process of this rearrangement of school function education would have been eliminated but, if no one said anything about it, it is doubtful that it would be missed.

In order to placate a worrisome public, the school would probably have to label some of the child care activities as "science experiences," "citizenship experiences," "nature study," "our heritage," and so on. There would be no harm in this so long as nothing was done differently on account of the labeling—so long, that is, as the child-care workers continued to pursue their job of providing interesting resources and activities for children without regard to the children's getting anything in particular out of them. Former teachers would no doubt be uneasy at first, but they would be reassured as it became evident that the children were not perceptibly more ignorant or less socialized than children who had been "educated."

The weak spot in this simple plan is the first step. Many teachers would object violently to having themselves recategorized as child-care workers or trainers. Either one sounds like a demotion, and it is. One could perhaps disguise the fact by inventing more impressive titles, but it is the case, curiously, that when you divide the teaching role into its subcomponents of child care and training neither seems to call for the high level of professional competence that teaching does.

There are two reasons I can see that teaching has a higher status than its component roles. The first is a legitimate one that has been suggested in the previous discussion. Child care and training are both rather simple, straightforward jobs; what is difficult and anomalous and what therefore seems to require a high level of professional sophistication is to do both jobs at once. The other reason derives from the mystique of education. The perennial calls for greatness that one hears in keynote addresses at teachers' conventions are not calls for people who are great at child tending or at teaching children to do fractions; they are calls for greatness in developing character, intellect, and citizenship. By separating teaching into child care and training we not only divide a difficult job into two easy ones, we also eliminate a fictitious third job, that of educator, which is the one that commands the prestige.

I don't wish to imply that child care and skill training are jobs that require no talent. Clearly a good child-care worker needs to be strong on human qualities, to relate well to children, to possess tact, patience, imagination, etc. On the other hand, it is doubtful if a child-care worker needs any special knowledge other than what may be acquired readily from those who already know the ropes. A good trainer does need some specialized skill in training techniques, perhaps in ways of gaining and holding attention, and so forth. But the formal part of such training could be accomplished by any person of average intelligence in a matter of a few weeks. In his highly successful Follow-Through model, Engelmann does just this, teaching low-income parents to function as trainers in language, reading, and arithmetic. They do the same work as professional teachers and are reportedly as effective. Another example comes from CIDOC, in Cuernavaca, where Ivan Illich uses young nonprofessionals as language teachers. In both cases the trainers use a highly structured program that minimizes the curricular decisions they have to make.

In the long run, a sensible staffing model for elementary schools would be one that had something like two professional child care specialists and one professional training specialist for every three hundred children. The rest of the staff could consist of nonprofessional adults working full-time or part-time, and adolescents working as part of a work-study program. It might be noted that summer camps manage to function successfully on a leaner model than this, with less professional guidance, but with quality child care and effective training being carried out by a staff of young counselors.

There is some logic to the staffing ratios I have proposed. The professional training specialist does not need to know the children in the school personally, but he needs to know the trainers and to work with them very closely in perfecting the training programs. Ideally, he ought also to have full authority to hire and fire them and himself be accountable for the successes and failures of training. The need for some professional supervision of child care is sufficiently obvious that it need not be spelled out. What I think is important is that the people who exercise supervision should be personally acquainted with the children involved. When this is not the case—as it often is not when schools make use of itinerant psychologists, psychiatrists, or child developmentalists—the situation becomes one that encourages outrageous irresponsibility and caprice on the part of the specialists.

Having the bulk of the work of running a school done by nonprofessionals has abundant advantages. In the first place, nonprofessionals, having little or no investment in preparation for the job, can be let go from it without its being a catastrophe. There is no shortage of the talents needed for child care and training, but some people don't have them. Under present conditions the removal of incompetent teachers is not only difficult for humane and contractual reasons but also because those who have the authority to fire teachers don't work with them closely enough to know which ones are incompetent. For trainers, the lack of a professional self-image would be a decided advantage. It would allow them to follow a prescriptive training program without feeling that they were lowering themselves, and this is a critical factor when it comes to implementing structured programs in schools. Finally, the use of nonprofessionals in child care would allow for a great deal more variety than does the use of professional teachers; it would include people with talents in different arts, and also people of different levels of maturity—from elderly ones down to those young enough to enter into the children's activities as participants rather than as directors or onlookers.

The result of these proposals would be that the elementary school teacher as we now know her would cease to exist, being replaced on one hand by somewhat more highly qualified professionals and on the other hand by a variety of nonprofessional workers. It does seem that the role of elementary school teacher is an outdated survival from the time of the one-room schoolhouse, when the disparate functions of child care and training had to be consolidated into one for the sake of economy.

The kind of school I have described may sound disunified. Perhaps it sounds even chaotic, but it should not be that. An overall administrative plan, perhaps on the model of a summer camp, with counselors continually responsible for small groups of children, could ensure a sufficiently orderly life in school. But disunified it would be. There would not be a coherent purpose, such as the educational goal of "developing the whole child."

Such a school could be a useful and an enjoyable place, but not a very important one. Many children could afford to stay away from it most of the time without loss. This sounds like a serious comedown from a grand ideal but, if you look at schools as they are and at the people who operate them, it seems that a less grandiose role is fitting. School people are for the most part worthwhile people for children to be around; but they are not people who should be carrying the burden of mankind's destiny, a burden with which they are not at all comfortable. And it should not require such an enormous bureaucratic establishment to fulfill the humble functions of the school.

The hordes of supervisors, consultants, and specialists who dominate our schools thrive upon a fantastic belief in the importance of what goes on in school. Neither the free school people, the English infant school people, nor the "return to fundamentals" people are doing anything to lessen this belief. Instead, the schools keep getting renewed calls for greatness from all sides. If we want schools to be brought down to human scale, we need to conceive a role for them that is also of human scale—a modest role that ordinary people can handle by themselves. To conceive of such a modest role is to conceive of schools without education.

chapter seven

A Better Life for Children

Child care must involve something more than being a shepherd. There has to be some concern for the quality of the life children are living, and this means that in some fashion adult values will be brought to bear on children. Resources for children's activities must be chosen and provided. The role of the child-care worker must be defined—what sort of influence, if any, the worker is to exert over children's behavior. Thus the whole question of education is reopened.

We need to consider the issues of resources and responsibilities in some depth. There is no reason why resources for children's activities should consist only of what is presently available. Current resources, after all, have been developed for a world in which children spend most of their active time in school. Nor can we take the baby-sitter as a model of the child-care worker's role. The baby sitter is a marginal figure, whereas the child-care worker, at least as I envision such a person, would be a major participant in children's lives.

The problems in providing a good life for children are not novel ones, but they look different when viewed from other than an educational perspective. The old criteria are gone. Most people, I find, are alarmed at the idea of ceasing to educate children because all they see as an alternative is letting them have fun. Just "letting them have fun" is not a realistic alternative at all. Choices have to be made of what resources to make available to children, and "fun" is not limiting enough to be a sufficient criterion. Children themselves often desire to do something worthwhile, and look for direction. And it is inconceivable that responsible adults could be found in large numbers who would be willing to inhibit any attempt whatever to influence children's choices of activities. It goes against nature.

What is needed is a new criterion, something other than an educational one, for deciding among possibilities. The criterion I want to explore in this chapter is that of improving the quality of immediate experience.

Quality of Experience

Let us begin the investigation by considering negative examples. There are a number of things children do that thoughtful adults frequently disapprove of: Little League sports, most television programs—most situation comedies, give-away shows, and melodramas with violent themes,—Barbie-dolls and other consumption-oriented playthings, war toys, and hanging around on street corners with nothing to do.

These amusements are generally criticized on educational grounds, for the effects they are feared to have on children's development. It is claimed they will make children grimly competitive, tasteless, acquisitive, cruel, unappreciative, materialistic, aimless, militaristic, and so on. These claims are difficult to support. What they show more than anything else is our education-mindedness, our concern with influencing how people turn out.

If we look behind the educational claims, however, we find them preceded by a more personal reaction: distaste, or moral revulsion. We simply don't like those television shows and those commercial toys, and we wish our children didn't like them either. When we discover that our children do like them, we try to come up with reasons why they are bad for the children. What we might do, instead, is to stick with our original feelings and act upon those. But on what grounds?

Let us look at the original list again and see the basis for our objections. Not all adults, of course, object to the amusements I have named. If they did we would not see so much of them. Those who do object to these amusements see more to them than meets the eye. With Little League sports, they see that the children, although highly involved, are often not having real fun and are, moreover, being used by adults for the adults' own needs. With the situation comedies they see a false picture of life which offends them and a low level of humor which they deplore. With the give-away shows they see greedy contestants sucking up to masters of ceremonies who show contempt and try to humiliate them to the delight of an audience jealous of the prizes the contestants are getting through no merit of their own. I could go on, but the important point has already been made. Adults judge children's experiences by their own esthetic and moral standards.

These standards are sometimes inappropriate, but not always. An adult needs to recognize that what is crude to him may be subtle to a child and [illegible] is banal, may be novel; conversely, what is clever to him ma[illegible] incomprehensible to the child, what is subtle may be flat, and w[illegible]te may be sissified. But on the other hand, what is cruel is [illegible]hat is cynically exploitative is cynically exploitative; and w[illegible] false is false. An adult's judgment on these matters may be wro[illegible] it is not irrelevant. A child may not see the cruelty, exploitatio[illegible]niness, but if they are there they are there.

One criterion for children's activi[illegible] meet adult moral standards. Why? No[illegible] quire the adults' standards, but because [illegible]be expected to have a part in things that he c[illegible]reprehensible.

Adults who are involved in the care of child[illegible]e a right, I would claim, to insist on honesty, decency, reaso[illegible]ble levels of taste, some imagination, some flair in what is provided to the young, without having to claim that the young profit from such things or are debased by their opposites. That adults will differ in their judgments goes without saying, but such differences do not invalidate the claim. What *does* present a serious problem is that, in acting on his moral judgments, the adult is imposing his values on children and thus appears to be functioning as an educator, whether he calls himself one or not.

There is no easy way out of this dilemma, but there is, I think, a difficult way out—difficult because it requires walking a narrow line between the present and the future. Imagine five children, each engaged in a different activity. One is watching a TV comedy. Another is gluing together a plastic model of Frankenstein. Another is reading Huckleberry Finn. Another is building a tree house out of old boards. The last is playing street hockey with his friends. Why do we feel that the last three are better occupied than the first two?

We can, of course, devise educational reasons, but it is quite possible that all five children are learning something worthwhile. I would suggest that there is a more profound difference to which most of us are sensitive, although seldom consciously so. The difference is that in what they are doing the last three children are more fully alive, more fully human, more fully themselves. It is not simply that they are more active in an objective sense, for the child gluing the model is more active than the one reading Huckleberry Finn.

Let me put it this way: One can imagine a lesser species of hominoid—something midway between a human being and an ape—for which following TV comedies and assembling precut plastic models would represent its highest attainments, not only intellectually and manually but, if you will, spiritually as well. If it could read, it could not experience Huckleberry Finn. If it could build, it could not create a design. If it could hit a ball with a stick, it could not play a team game. Although these last three activities are not the height of man's capabilities, they are a step in that direction beyond the first two. By such a criterion, I think, we are entitled to judge them more worthy of a child's time. And on this basis we would be justified in encouraging a child who was watching television or assembling a model to try one of the other activities.

Is that kind of encouragement education? It depends on your definition. I prefer to say it is not, because the encouragement is only concerned with present experience and not with future development. John Dewey, who built his theory of education around the idea of experience, always maintained that education required selecting experiences on the basis of their possibilities for future development. What I am suggesting has a good deal of consonance with Dewey's view, but it is purely contemporaneous. It is not concerned with the person that the child is becoming but with the person that he is right now, with actualizing the humanity that is already there.

To encourage children to express, through their activities, the best that is in them, is to impose a value. It is not just any value, however. To me it is the one value that people who care about each other cannot help but impose. And if there is one irreducible requirement of child care, it is that it must involve real caring.

Cultural Resources for Children

Children are in school only about half the days of the year. What society provides for children's activities the rest of the time is designed mainly to complement the school and consists mainly of playgrounds. Considering what school life has traditionally been like, it isn't unreasonable that out-of-school resources should provide physical play and amusement. The needs of the mind are presumably taken care of by school.

If schools are abandoned, however, or if when they give up their educational efforts children start spending less time in them, then the existing resources will no longer be adequate. Experimental schools can find ample resources for children out in the community, but imagine what it would be like if all the children in a city were taken out on the town. More resources would have to be created, of more diverse kinds; but presumably there would be more money to create them if less money went into schooling.

In this section I will consider possible new resources that would take the place of schooling rather than merely complement it. I hope the basic idea of creating alternative resources will not be judged by the quality of my specific suggestions. I am an educationist by trade, and the first thing that needs to be realized is that educationists are not the people to look to for noneducational alternatives to schooling. There are all kinds of other people in the fields of the arts, sciences, engineering, and media who could have a great deal to offer if they were not expected to produce things educational. Educationists could make a contribution to planning, because of their down-to-earth experience in working with children in groups, but they are also limited in their talents and vision.

1. Intellectual recreation

Schools have claimed a virtual monopoly on the intellectual life of children. Television programs like Sesame Street have now begun to challenge this monopoly, but interestingly enough they are moving in to compensate for the schools' failures in training. There is not much intellectual play in school, except where the occasional teacher has a liking for it. That is changing. Teachers appear to be showing an increasing interest in intellectual games. But in many a classroom all the intellectual play is carried out behind the teacher's back: children exchange riddles, play tic-tac-toe behind their textbooks, pass on puzzles, and last but not least devise all kinds of devious games in which the teacher is the unwitting goat.

Recreational centers provide for physical and social fun. I can see a place for comparable recreational centers concerned with intellectual fun. Much intellectual recreation, of course, can arise spontaneously, without special facilities. But still there would be value in having places where children with intellectual interests could meet each other; where game equipment, books, journals, scientific devices, and the like would be available; where puzzles and interesting clippings would be pinned to the walls; where competitions, fairs, and simulation games would be organized; and where intellectually stimulating adults would be around for children to interact with.

It is quite conceivable that such centers would do more for children's general intellectual development than schools do now. But they would not be judged by such effects and one would have to be wary of directors who began to think of their establishments as mental training camps.

2. Resources that encourage doing

Social critics often bemoan the trend toward more spectator amusements. They imply that modern man has gotten slack and dispirited, mesmerized by his color TV. It is often suggested that education must do something about this creeping passivity. I would suggest, however, that the cause is not to be found in man's sagging nature but in the enormously increased ease of access to spectator amusements. It takes almost no determination to switch on a television set, whereas starting to play squash or to do *papier-mâché* sculpture is a major undertaking. Doing can not, by its nature, be made as convenient or easy as watching, but barriers can be removed.

Organized participant activities in our society are, by and large, extremely forbidding to the incompetent and the uninitiated. An in-group tends to develop around each activity, develops its own procedures, its own lingo, its subtle ways of discouraging outsiders. It also naturally develops its standards of competence that put the beginner in a humiliating position. As a result the only people who last long enough to make it to the in-group are the bold, the very determined, the naturally talented, or the ones who have a friend to support them. One of the advantages of the common school is that a child does not have to earn a place in it; he is there by assignment, like a draftee in the armed forces. If schooling is replaced with voluntary activities, and if nothing is done to change the social dynamics of such activities, there is going to be a problem with children who simply can't make it—the shy, the inept, the friendless, the unaggressive—children who will be inclined to withdraw to the safety of the television set.

There is a job of social engineering to be done. What is required is not educating people to be bolder or more accepting but redesigning organized participant activities to make them more hospitable. There are ways that have shown some promise—for instance, the buddy system. When a child has indicated an interest in getting into something like a theater group, someone already in the group is assigned to him, gets acquainted with him and counsels him before he ever shows up at a meeting, and then shepherds him through the early stages of his assimilation into the group.

3. Quiet places

Philip W. Jackson has pointed out that crowding is an outstanding feature of classroom life.[1] For the poor, crowding is a feature of home life as well. Children should have places to go when they want quiet and freedom from social stimulation. Public libraries have

[1] Jackson, *Life in Classrooms.*

provided such a place, although for a rather specialized clientele. Now even that is changing as libraries become media centers that encourage bustle and social interaction. What has happened to the librarians who used to hiss "Shush!"? Perhaps we could find reemployment for them in new kinds of institutions where quiet prevailed but where there was no particular thing that children were supposed to do—where they could read or draw or sew or dream or engage in tête-a-têtes provided they did not rise above a murmur. It would also be nice if such places could provide booths for privacy, although I honestly don't know how that could work.

4. Age intermixing

The segregation of children according to age is largely due to graded curricula in schools. Outside there are natural age groupings according to interests and abilities, but they are much looser. There is no reason that child care should be rigidly age-segregated. Indeed, there are interesting opportunities for enriching experience by bringing together people of varied ages—the young and the elderly, for instance, who have in common the fact that they have an abundance of free time.

Disneyland is perhaps the most striking proof that something successfully designed to appeal to children will also appeal to adults. The exception is activities that are exclusively educational. It is no fun to be taught things you already know. One practical advantage of designing things that appealed to both adults and children is that they could be made partly self-financing by making the adults pay.

More important, however, would be finding ways to get children, youths, old people, and poor people into activities that are presently dominated by adults who can pay: amateur drama and music groups, photography clubs, sporting clubs, art associations, archaeology and nature clubs, and the like. To make such groups less exclusive would be to turn them more into family and community organizations. Yet it would be well to maintain the nucleus of able, committed people who currently make up such groups.

One way to accomplish this would be through subsidized age integration. Adults certainly have a right to separate themselves off from children; expert chess players have a right not to bother playing with beginners. But such exclusiveness is a luxury they should expect to pay for, as they do now. Probably many adult groups would be willing to make a place for those currently excluded if they were subsidized in a reasonable amount for it. This would be cheaper than constructing Golden Age clubs and community centers and would be a step toward restoring some of the continuity of life that was lost with the breakdown of the extended family.

5. User-programmed facilities

The Illich-Reimer distinction, noted in chapter 5, between manipulative or authoritarian institutions on one hand and convivial or democratic institutions on the other may be applied to cultural facilities. A bowling alley is authoritarian. It programs its users. Everything you do is prescribed and scheduled. The equipment can only be used for one purpose and only in the intended way. A pond, on the other hand, is democratic. Unless a park authority imposes a lot of restrictions, all sorts of people can use it in all sorts of ways. You can paddle a canoe over it, cool beer bottles in it, or delight your toes by wading in the mud along its banks.

There is a place in life for both bowling alleys and ponds. What is needed is balance, and the balance seems to be shifting unhappily toward facilities that program the users. Designing user-programmed facilities requires some art. Modern science museums try to involve the user, and they contain many clever displays, but mostly they are ones where you read a little sign and then do what it tells you.

I remember an exhibit at a technological museum in Amsterdam where a number of bottles of sand kept circulating around a conveyor that sorted them into full, half-full, and quarter-full, and then mixed them together again, the sorting being done by little electric eyes at appropriate heights to gauge the fullness of the bottles. My son and I found that by inserting a card to block the light to an electric eye just at the moment a bottle was passing, we could cause the machine to sort wrongly. We amused ourselves happily confusing the machine, until a guard came along and indicated that a sign in Dutch above the machine was forbidding just what we were doing. Here was a case of accidental programming by the user resulting from our inability to read the sign that was intended to program the user.

There are already a number of nonmanipulative devices available for young children—jungle gyms, housekeeping corners, and much of the nursery school equipment from houses like Creative Playthings. For older children, however, there is not much. I don't see why there should be any greater difficulty in designing nonmanipulative devices for them. It is simply an undeveloped area of technology.

Who Decides?

Creating a new government bureaucracy charged with ministering to the cultural life of children is not a very attractive prospect. It would look too much like the existing educational establishment and would be subject to the same objections of invading the sphere of individual freedom. On the other hand, leaving it to a consumer market is not a very satisfactory solution either. The television wasteland should convince us of that. There ought to be a way for really creative ideas for design of the environment and for cultural activities to gain a foothold and not invariably be wiped out by mass tastes.

There is some hope in group decisions. Get a representative panel of ordinary citizens together to decide what should be offered on television, and I think you would get something of a higher quality than is offered now. The reason is that an individual's tastes are not defined as a point on a scale but as a range of things that he will find interesting, meaningful, valuable. In a consumer market things tend to gravitate to the low end of the range. Brought together to consider seriously what they want, people will tend to choose toward the high end. If I am right in this expectation—and I have only a little informal experience to base it on—then democratic decisions over the years should lead to a gradual upgrading of the quality of cultural resources.

Group decisions, however, tend to be conservative and unimaginative (even when the groups are composed of radicals). There are, fortunately, some policies that can counteract this tendency, if groups have the good sense to follow them. A time-honored one is design competitions. Decision-making groups would do well to hold very unconstrained competitions for ideas and designs to create a richer environment for children. Ideas could come from many sources, not the least of which is children. After all, if high school students can design space experiments for NASA they should be able to come up with some worthwhile things for themselves. To this end it would be well to have children on any decision-making panel, if only to help insure that ideas from other children were given a serious hearing.

The other policy is to award small grants indiscriminately. Such a policy was recently implemented in Canada. Called the Local Initiatives Program, it doled out money to an enormous variety of individually proposed projects of some putative social value that would provide short-term jobs to unemployed people. As a result, some neighborhood craft centers were established, a barn was fixed up for use by an "awareness" group, and I know not what else. What is impressive about this approach is that even if a majority of the projects are worthless, the few good things that result are worth the total cost, which is more than can be said for grand efforts like the War on Poverty or the Right to Read program.

To summarize, what I am proposing is a modest populist approach to the creation of cultural resources for children. If money can be pried loose from the schools it should not be put into the hands of another bureaucracy to administer according to some official conception of the public good. It ought to be put into the hands of a body representing the interests of parents and children, a body that would recognize its own limitations and that would accordingly be responsive to the ideas of competing designers and would be relatively indiscriminate in the awarding of small grants to people who had things they wanted to do. This would not provide a quick route to a golden age, but at least it would get people to think and try to do something about the quality of the lives they lead, which is something that our educational system has never been able to do.

Child-Care Workers

We have been talking about cultural resources for children. These could be resources out in the community or resources within the walls of what are currently called schools. The child-care worker is the person who brings children into contact with these resources, looking after their welfare in the process, and who tries to help children get the most out of those resources. There can be different kinds of child-care workers—male and female, young and old, permissive and demanding, and they can have a variety of tastes and skills and come from a variety of backgrounds. For that reason parents and children need some choice and some way to find out what they are getting. I don't think it is important here to go into administrative details on this point. General principles should suffice.

What is important is to define the role of child-care worker, to distinguish it from that of the teacher on one hand and the baby sitter on the other. The role of the teacher is to educate—to steer development along a course deemed favorable. That is a role I have been questioning throughout this book. The role of the baby sitter I see as an essentially negative one. It is to keep anything unfortunate from happening to the children during the brief period of her responsibility for them.

The role of the child-care worker is to increase the quality of children's immediate experience, to help them be more fully themselves in the present moment. Thus the child-care worker is a kind of experience specialist. This is a new role, although it has some parallels in the role of the tour guide, the art critic, and the television sports announcer. From these parallels we can see what some of the dangers of the role are. It can easily lapse into the role of the teacher—as seen in the tour guide who becomes a teacher of art history, sometimes of the most pedantic sort. Or the person can try to become a showman or an artist in his own right: the tour guide becomes the main exhibit; the art critic becomes an essayist trying to focus attention on his own ideas rather than on the thing he is discussing; the sportscaster becomes entertainer, using the game as a prop. Or the person may use his role to service his own needs—his vanity, his need for affection, or what not.

Child-care workers, being human, would be susceptible to all these perversions. There is nothing wrong with wanting to teach, to perform, or to seek affection. It is only if these urges prevent the child-care worker from doing his job that they become serious. The most dangerous is the urge to shape children. Not to make them behave, which is a matter of dealing sensibly with the present situation, but to shape the course of their future development. A child-care worker needs to tolerate a wide range of individual differences. If he thinks every child ought to be sociable and outgoing, he is likely to end up teaching extraversion.

Would child-care workers need to be trained? To a limited extent, perhaps. Like any job, child care has techniques that are worth passing on in an organized form. But I do not see the need for any elaborate or lengthy preparation. Rather, it would be important to establish clear expectations of the job to be done and to weed out people who could not or would not meet those expectations. I have only defined those expectations in the most general way. More specific expectations could best be worked out in practice, by observing people who were models of what an experience specialist should and should not be.

As I think of possible models for the experience specialist, my mind turns to someone I have lunch with occasionally. He does not stand out as a sophisticated diner but he has the ability to absorb an unusual amount of experience from the simple occasion of going to a neighborhood restaurant and, somehow, to share this experience with those around him. He does this with a minimum of explanation but with a great deal of self-expression and "relating" to things, events, and people. It is significant that he does not expect other people to be like him. He wants to share his enthusiasms with them, but he does not pressure them to become, like him, an enthusiast.

This is one worthy kind of experience specialist. Others might be more given to verbalization, to questioning and speculation; others might be more oriented toward action, toward mobilizing group undertakings; others might be more disposed to passive witnessing. Any of these could contribute to a fuller life for children, without imposing developmental goals on children in any way.

chapter eight

Optional Adolescence

Childhood, like senility, is a biological state of dependency. There will always be a need for child care, as there will always be a need for care of those incapacitated by old age. Adolescence is more like retirement. It is a conferred social status that keeps a person out of the work force, regardless of his capabilities.

Both adolescence and retirement are conferred arbitrarily on people of a certain age, and hence they are liable to be unjust impositions, contrary to the needs of the individual. But we should not overgeneralize. Some people welcome retirement and the freedom it brings from the daily grind of earning a living. For these people the loss of income that usually goes with retirement is more than compensated by the opportunity to relax and enjoy life, to travel, to pursue hobbies, and to engage in social activities that are impossible for the fulltime employed. But for others retirement means only poverty, boredom, loneliness, and loss of purpose. It means exclusion from the main activity that has given meaning to their lives.

The same differences may be observed in adolescence (indeed, it may be the same kinds of people who benefit from or suffer from both adolescence and retirement). For some people the period of adolescent freedom from responsibility is a valuable time in which they can explore life, experiment with life styles, work out a personal identity and set of values, and pursue nonlucrative occupations such as the arts. It is a time when many people strive seriously to acquire knowledge and to develop their potentialities. It is a time when some people pursue idealistic and even dangerous causes that they could not pursue when saddled with adult responsibilities.

So much for the romance of youth. There is also a vast number of people for whom adolescence, like retirement, means mainly poverty, boredom, loneliness and lack of purpose. It is these people that writers like Goodman and Musgrove have had in mind when they proposed doing away with adolescence and letting people move directly from childhood into adult roles.[1]

Does it not appear obvious that the sensible solution is neither to impose adolescence on everyone nor do away with it, but to make adolescence optional? It seems obvious to me, and therefore puzzling that social thinkers should be trying to find a single solution to fit everyone.

Different Ways to Spend the Adolescent Years

Trow and Clark have identified four quite different orientations among college students.[2] The first is the *academic,* characterized by serious pursuit of education in learned disciplines. Although liberal arts curricula are aimed at students with this orientation, only a minority of students in these curricula actually have it. The second orientation is *collegiate,* and centers around social life—having fun, participating in fraternities or sororities, campus social activities, and collegiate sports, either as a player or a fan. This orientation would appear to be less prevalent now than it used to be, but it can still be observed in full flower by watching television on any Saturday afternoon in the football season. The third orientation is called *nonconformist.* The nonconformist student uses adolescent freedom mainly for self-discovery and personal pursuits. He is interested in learning, but in informal ways—through reading, conver-

[1] Paul Goodman, *Growing Up Absurd* (New York: Random House, 1960); Frank Musgrove, *Youth and the Social Order* (Bloomington, Ind.: Indiana University Press, 1965).

[2] Martin Trow and B. R. Clark, unpublished research cited in L. S. Lewis, "The Value of College to Different Subcultures," *School Review* 77 (1969): 32–40.

sation, and direct experience—rather than through formal study, which he is likely to see as "interfering with his education." The last orientation is *vocational,* characterized by an interest in qualifying for a career and in attaining upward social mobility. Learning is only a means to this end, and any learning that doesn't obviously serve that end is likely to be regarded as worthless.

To these four orientations we might add two others that are more common among young people who do not go to college. One is the *common man* orientation, to use the British term. This is orientation toward a working-class job or marriage, following in the footsteps of one's parents. To young people with this orientation adolescence is at best a brief period of transition for finding a spot or finding a mate; if further extended, adolescence becomes only a delay. Finally, there is the *delinquent* orientation, characterized by hostility to the surrounding society, a lack of purpose, and unwillingness to give in to the demands of adult life. Adolescence becomes a period of delaying eventual resignation to those demands and settling into an unrewarding life of work and parenthood.

These six orientations, I would suggest, are all legitimate, given life as it is, although some of them are unfortunate. An adequate set of options for young people ought to allow for all of these orientations. The following constitute a minimum set of options.

1. Liberal studies

For the minority of students with an academic orientation, I would see something patterned more after the small liberal arts college and the graduate school than after the high school and the large undergraduate university. The latter serve masses of students, most of whom do not have a serious interest in academic pursuits. They fail on several important counts to meet the needs of academically oriented youth. As mass producers of learning, these institutions don't provide the quality or intensity of teaching that is needed. Courses are watered down and there is not much chance for close interaction between a scholar and a learner. Furthermore the high schools, at least, fail because they are too vulnerable to political pressures to permit honest intellectual inquiry in socially sensitive areas.

What I am proposing is true education for a minority of students. If it is carried out within independent centers of higher learning like our better liberal arts colleges and graduate schools, it can be relatively free of the dangers of imposing public values on individual learners. There is, first of all, a tradition of academic freedom that permits teachers to pursue lines of instruction and inquiry that are critical of prevailing norms; there is generally a wide choice of courses and teachers open to students—and then one is dealing with students of an age and an intellectual caliber such that they are in a position to respond intelligently to educational influences and to make up their own minds. I see this kind of education as a form of apprenticeship in learned disciplines rather than as a method of forming personalities.

2. Unrestricted adolescence

The majority of students who now go to college are not academically oriented, and yet going to college is not a total waste for them. Most of what they get out of college, however, comes not from the curriculum but from association with fellow students and, to a lesser extent, with faculty members. The faculty members who are most valuable to them are not generally the most serious scholars but are the ones who share an interest in student concerns, in social action, and in self-discovery—the ones that Peter Berger calls "honorary youths." Academic course work may have some value in bringing students into contact with ideas and criticism, but mostly it is a kind of penalty they have to pay for the privilege of spending four years in a college environment. For many students the penalty is too severe. They either drop out or else they have to work so hard to survive academically that they do not have time for the informal activities that would be more rewarding to them. This is especially likely to be true of students who come from less literate backgrounds and who lack the skills that would permit them to take academic work in their stride.

It would seem immensely more sensible and humane to allow this large group of young people to enjoy their adolescence without the burden of formal academic work. All they need is money. Some young people are already managing this sort of thing. They manage to drop out of school without letting their parents find out, and thus continue for a while as campus hangers-on while living off the parental allowance. Or they congregate in communes and scrape by, sharing the occasional money that someone picks up from a job or a gift or from begging or from selling homemade candles. Sometimes they even manage to organize informal seminars, under the rubric of the "free university," to provide the kind of learning experience that is most meaningful to them. Their seminars on witchcraft and revolution may look ridiculous by academic standards, but they are a step up from unfocussed bull sessions.

In order for unrestricted adolescence to be available to everyone who might want it, society would have to be willing to pay for it. Society is a long way from that now. In order for a student to receive a scholarship or a loan he has to shoulder the burden of a full academic program and handle it successfully. The ideal arrangement would be to give every citizen the right to a certain number of years on welfare—say four years—without the obligation of accepting employment if it is available. A person would then have the option of using welfare funds for unrestricted adolescence or using it later to take "sabbaticals" from his work, whatever it might be.

A more acceptable arrangement might be to award unrestricted grants during the years up to age twenty-one that could be used for academic pursuits or for doing nothing in particular. These grants would be paid back in later years by a surtax on income. This arrangement would have the advantage of ultimately paying for itself, but in a way that would not overburden those with low incomes. (It would of course, require tax reform, but the reforms are already needed. If grant money had to be recovered through income tax, this might provide a spur for tax reforms to close loopholes that enable the wealthiest to escape taxation.)

3. Service corps

This option, which has been advocated by Paul Goodman, would provide a chance for youths to do significant work in the company of peers, often away from parents. Service corps work would generally not take the place of existing jobs. There is a great deal of work that needs to be done in the world that is not being done because there is no way for private enterprise to make a profit from it and it is too expensive to be carried out at public expense at ordinary rates of pay. There is work concerned with restoration and beautification of the environment. There is public day care for children which, at rates of $1500 or more per year per child, is simply impractical. But most of the cost is in labor, and a service corps that could maintain young workers economically would lower such costs appreciably. Services of these kinds would provide worthwhile work for many of the less talented of young people.

In addition, however, there is a wealth of talent among the young—talent in music, in decoration, in crafts, in planning, in research, and in work with people—that could be applied in various ways to raising the quality of life. I don't want to go into details, but I would suggest to the reader the following exercise for bringing possibilities to mind: Think of any place you have been in the last day and consider ways in which the place or the things that went on in it might have been made better—more convivial, more productive, more democratic in its benefits—and I think you will be able to imagine ways in which young people might have been able to make a significant contribution.

I think of a subway ride across Toronto—a pleasant enough experience already, compared to subway rides in other North American cities I know. But I could imagine the following: roving musicians, as sometimes found on Mexican buses; guides at the major transfer points to help unsophisticated travelers find their way; art to beautify the subway stations and to give some character to the subway cars; social centers at the ends of certain subway cars where you could go if you wanted to talk to strangers during your transit; a portable heater in the chillier subway stations where you could warm your hands and eat a freshly roasted chestnut. All of these are possible at little expense, except that they would take a bit of labor and a bit of talent. Service corps workers could provide it, and I think it would end up doing something grand for the quality of life in Toronto, which is big on decency but low on human warmth.

4. Vocational training, apprenticeship, on-the-job training, and work

James S. Coleman has very tellingly pointed out the limitations of formal schooling as a way of teaching people the skills needed for getting along in adult life.[3] He has proposed that the education of adolescents be largely taken away from schools and put in the hands of the economic institutions in which adults spend their lives. The main fault in this proposal is that it would mean consigning adolescents to be schooled in the ethic of economic growth and corporate loyalty which many people see as socially disastrous. Still, people must acquire job skills and most of them will come to terms with the corporate way of life one way or other. The interests of vocationally oriented youth, in short, need to be respected and met.

But the interests of vocationally oriented youth do not necessarily have to be met at public expense or through public ministration. High schools and technical colleges are now doing a lot of industry's work. They are providing vocational training and, perhaps more importantly, they are carrying out a very expensive process of sorting young people into various categories of employability. The general high school diploma no longer means much as a mark of learning. It merely means that a person has demonstrated over several years a fair degree of persistence and conformity to work demands, and thus it is not surprising that industries should require high school diplomas for many kinds of jobs that do not require any learning.

Ivar Berg, in his exhaustive study titled, *Education and Jobs: The Great Training Robbery,* has shown that public schools do not do a very good job of either training or sorting.[4] The training often proves to be irrelevant to actual employment. And school success is not a very good predictor of job performance. This is not so much a fault of the schools as it is the fault of a system whereby a general-purpose institution tries to prepare people for employment in a variety of special-purpose institutions.

By the withdrawal of public schools from the vocational training business, industry would be required to assume responsibility for training its workers. Already, it is estimated, industry spends almost as much on education as is spent in the public sector, and so this shift of responsibility would not be revolutionary. It would mean

[3] J. S. Coleman, "How Do the Young Become Adults?" *Phi Delta Kappan* 54 (1972): 226–30.

[4] I. E. Berg, *Education and Jobs: The Great Training Robbery* (New York: Praeger Publishers, Inc., 1970).

more efficient and relevant training. It would also mean that young people could be working and earning something while they learned.

There would still be a place for school-type vocational training for people who needed rehabilitation or who wanted to switch careers. The fairest way to handle this would be through a system of entitlements or vouchers, that people could draw upon at any time—not only when they are young—and that they could use in private training schools. These schools thrive now, without subsidies, apparently because they give people what they need when they need it, without a lot of surplus educational baggage. I refer to secretarial schools, computer programming schools, foreign language schools, and the like. Given a capitalistic system, it seems to make more sense to have vocational training be part of it rather than part of a public institution that has an ambiguous loyalty, divided between public interests on one hand and private interests on the other.

Another reason for placing vocational training in the private sector is to avoid making the definition of competence a public issue. The outcome of a vocational training course is a certificate that testifies to some sort of competence. You can also, for some purposes, get your competence certified without training by going to a vocational testing service. If schooling requirements become illegal as a basis for employment (as one Supreme Court decision promises to make them—see chapter 3), there will be a greatly increased need for such certification. Now if certification is handled through private concerns the certificates will be worth their market value—much or little depending on the reputation of the concern. But if training and certification are handled publicly, we will inevitably have bureaucrats deciding what you need in order to be a good secretary or bricklayer and aspiring secretaries and bricklayers will have to toe the line no matter how meaningless or excessive it might be.

The marriage between the schoolhouse and the marketplace is not a satisfactory one. By dissolving it we would free young people to find their way in the marketplace according to their own lights. A person might seek early employment and learn on the job. Or he might take the option of some years of unrestricted adolescence, by the end of which he might have acquired by informal means some marketable skills that could be certified. Or, if not, he could, like many of the girls who now graduate from expensive liberal arts colleges and then take a secretarial course in order to obtain work, undertake some brief vocational training to secure entry into a particular career.

Providing for the Social Life of Adolescents

Hardly anyone has a good word to say for the high school. It is a baby-sitting institution for people who aren't babies anymore. In it young people who don't want to be there in the first place are subjected to boring courses and absurd parietal rules. Yet, paradoxically, the very worst high schools have to have guards at the doors —to keep people out!

Not everyone who wants to get into these high schools is a dope peddler. Many of them are dropouts who find that life on the outside is lonely and even more boring than life on the inside. In particular, many of them are boys who find that high school is the only place where there is much chance to associate with girls.

As an institution for meeting the social needs of adolescents the high school, for all its wretchedness, is peculiarly appropriate. Recreational centers, drive-ins, hamburger joints, and the like have their place, but they do not fulfill the main function nearly as well. They are too much like singles bars for adults. The issue of sexual availability is too much in the forefront. It frightens off the more timid, and creates too much tension among the bold to allow them to get to know each other in a relaxed fashion.

High school is a sort of coeducational work-place with hourly coffee breaks. There is nothing else quite like it. Classes provide a legitimate reason for boys and girls to congregate. Class activities provide legitimate occasions for them to interact. This sort of thing is especially important for children of the working class because of their more sharply distinguished sex roles. Working-class boys and girls do not have many interests in common and the kinds of jobs they can get are usually segregated by sex. It is unfortunate that high school is most significant socially for the people for whom it is the least appropriate academically.

The alternatives to high school that I have suggested in the preceding section do not take care of the social needs of a large part of the adolescent population. For the kinds of adolescents who now go to college, the options I have suggested should provide something better than the high school: longer coffee breaks, if you will. I would see something like the following emerging as a social structure. There would be small commuter colleges offering serious liberal arts courses for academically oriented young people from the age of thirteen or so onward, with larger centers of learning, patterned after graduate schools, to which they could move in later adolescence. None of these would be custodial institutions like our present high schools. Outside of class, students' lives would be their own. But these colleges and universities would also be places where less academically oriented youths could congregate—to take an occasional course, to participate in informal seminars, or just to hang around in student lounges and do as they pleased. There would not be a sharp line separating academic from nonacademic students. The academic students could take part in the more informal activities, as could the faculty members. Sexual intermixing would take place naturally in such settings, since there is no very sharp separation of interests between boys and girls of the kind who are drawn to this sort of life.

The losers would be working-class young people who were drawn into either service corps or vocational options. In either case they are likely to find themselves involved in activities that separate them from people of the opposite sex and also from people of different interests and abilities. In other words, they would face the same situation that they do now in the employment world, a situation that makes the working-class youth wistful for high school days.

It is difficult to imagine a solution that is not artificial. The high school, after all, is a very artificial solution, and one that provides its social benefits at high personal cost. My own feeling is that social interaction is not something that should be imposed on people. Service corps and vocational activities could be engineered with the specific objective of breaking down sexual and social boundaries, but I see that as an underhanded form of education, imposing middle-class liberal values on people who don't share them. After all, the lack of shared interests and abilities among working-class men and women is a condition closely tied to the way sex roles are defined in that segment of society. It is not a social problem to be solved. Social engineering, I think, ought to go only as far as seeing to it that institutionalized activities are not unwittingly engineered to produce segregation.

People, including young people, ultimately need to be responsible for their own forms of social interaction. If the labor world is too rigidly segregated, labor unions ought to concern themselves with that problem. Employers ought to be responsive to demands, but it isn't their job to decide how workers ought to relate to each other socially. Similarly, youth organizations like a service corps ought to be responsive to expressed social needs of young people and remain flexible in design so that, eventually, structures might evolve that would provide young people with the kinds of social life they seek; but they shouldn't set out to implement adult ideas of what that social life should be.

A Caste System?

The options I have suggested smack somewhat of an adolescent caste system in which the brains go to school; in which the children of the upper middle-class play, being confident of a good job when they feel ready; and in which the children of the poor haul stones. That is more or less what we have now, but mass education serves as something of a counterforce. A more distinctive set of options, on the other hand, might serve to strengthen social class divisions.

I suspect that in one way it would and in another, it wouldn't. The U.S. military force in Vietnam showed both tendencies. Basically a poor-man's army, it has driven a dangerous wedge between the working-class young who were fighting the war and the college youths who were protesting it. Indeed, we have seen bloody class warfare between the students and the police who, also working-class youths, functioned as a sort of home-front contingent of the army. On the other hand, the army in Vietnam served, as other armies have served, to bridge local and ethnic boundaries and thus to unite people to some extent. We could expect something of the same effect with a service corps, although in a more benign form.

Making more options available clearly makes it more possible for people to separate themselves from each other, but I think some of the worries on this account are unfounded. One of the concerns I have heard voiced is that the academic option would create an elitist educational system of the very kind that European countries are trying to get away from; that there would be tremendous competition to get into the academic courses; that well-schooled children of the wealthy would dominate them; and that graduates of them would in turn dominate society. In short, it would create a British-style upper class.

It would be unwise to discount this possibility entirely, but I don't think it is a very realistic possibility in present times. What we are talking about with an academic option is not the education of gentlemen but the education of intellectuals, scholars, and scientists. Such people are being educated now in our graduate schools. A few of them attain positions of power, but not very many, and I don't see any reason that the situation would change.

The rich and the powerful are much more likely to emerge from the ranks of nonacademically oriented youth who devote their adolescence to more practical kinds of action and self-development, and in this connection I see optional adolescence as much more democratic than elitist in its tendency. The British school system, as Musgrove has pointed out, makes access to leadership positions senselessly dependent on academic studiousness. This is true in America as well, even if not so blatantly. There is plenty of evidence that there exists a great reservoir of leadership talent among black Americans, but the only blacks who get a chance to use this talent in established institutions are the ones who happen also to be academically talented. By making adolescent freedom available outside the academic channel, there would be at least a few alternate routes by which adolescents might make their way into positions of influence in politics, business, and public service. Colleges are working toward such alternatives now, through special programs for black students, but the result tends to be ersatz higher education rather than truly meaningful alternatives.

Where the real danger of caste-like separation lies is between those who choose adolescence and those who choose work and marriage. The split is already well-formed. The old distinction between middle-class and lower-class becomes increasingly meaningless. The split is higher up, between the upper-middle-class and those beneath, and it is a split that pretty much divides those who go to college from those who don't. But that, I think, is incidental. College courses don't make the difference. What makes the difference, I believe, is whether or not people undergo an extended adolescence.

Traditional psychology has led us to believe that personality and values are formed in childhood, perhaps in very early childhood. Without denying the importance of the early years, however, one can find evidence that adolescence is another very important formative period, in which the individual is open to major changes. Nevitt Sanford and his colleagues, of whom I was one for a brief period, have explored the changes that can take place in late adolescence. In childhood the individual develops a kind of unconscious social self in relation to his parents and his peers. If all goes well he becomes adjusted to life in society as it is, a conformist. But in adolescence he becomes conscious of his own identity and of the tension between his personal wants and society's demands. He comes to identify with people beyond his immediate circle, to acquire personal and social ideals rather than conventional sentiments. To put it generally, he acquires a kind of personal and social integration that is more complex and individualized than he had before.

The person who becomes an adult at seventeen or eighteen—who settles directly into work and marriage—misses most of this period of development. For the person who goes to college, providing he does not follow a narrow vocationally oriented line, adolescence extends into the twenties and commonly produces a different sort of adult—perhaps a better one. Educators generally think so, and consequently favor extended adolescence for everyone in the form of schooling. I am more inclined to think that the world needs both kinds or that, in any event, it is not for us to make the judgment and impose it on one and all.

One hope I would entertain is that a service corps could become sufficiently challenging and rewarding that it would attract young people of all kinds, not just those who can find nothing better to do. As a public institution it would be limited in that it could engage only in relatively noncontroversial activities, and that would tend to keep out more radical youth. But with sufficient imagination it could still do a great deal that would be worthwhile in the eyes of idealistic and practical-minded youth. Unlike its counterparts such as the Civilian Conservation Corps, the Peace Corps, and the

Job Corps, it ought to be designed and managed by young people, like the Company of Young Canadians. It ought to remain continuously experimental, both in its programs and in its living arrangements, so that there were many real options within it and so that it changed with the times. The term "corps" is perhaps unfortunate, since the army is one of the poorest models it could imitate. (Don't ask me for a good model. Institutional design is not one of modern man's strong points. I once saw a good organization of neighbors for removing the contents of a burning house, but it only lasted for half an hour.) A service corps could become a truly democratic institution—one, for instance, in which the dirty work was not all done by flunkies or women, but was shared—that got young people of all kinds working together and living together. We should not expect a service corps to eliminate caste altogether; but if I am correct that we are already developing a caste system that has its origins in adolescence, then a balancing force in the direction of democracy ought to be welcome and worth some effort to establish.

Is Youth Too Dangerous to Be Free?

We keep children shut up in schools for their safety. In large degree we keep adolescents shut up in schools for *our* safety. Adolescents are frightening people. They are responsible for a lot of crime and for a lot of the carnage on highways. Around the world they are a threat to the established social order, especially if they are intelligent, unemployed, and out of school.

Accordingly it should not be surprising if adult society recoils from the idea of unrestricted adolescence, supporting young people to do nothing in particular. It is tantamount to supporting revolution or, at the very least, drug addiction and free love. From this alarmist point of view, schools are a necessity to keep young people in line. Even if schools do a poor job, it is better than turning the young people loose on society. And, it can be argued, schools do not do such a poor job, all things considered. True, it looked in the late 1960s as if the high schools and colleges were on the point of collapse; but they recovered, with a little help from a wave of unemployment, and that crisis only serves to show what a valuable function the schools regularly perform.

I am forced to acknowledge that there is some truth to the alarmist view. If you want a stable society, you have to put a damper on youth. You can do it through putting them to work or you can do it by committing them to institutions, of which the school is the most humane. Adolescence, after all, is a temporary condition and if you can keep the patient in check for a few years, no matter how you do it, he will generally experience spontaneous recovery and become a law-abiding adult.

But two observations are in order. The first is that the tide of history is running against all efforts at keeping young people in check. Even though adolescence is a temporary condition, adolescents constitute a subjugated group, like blacks and women, and they are bound to get their share of benefits from the movement toward equal rights. We are going to have to learn to live with them.

The other observation is that in putting a damper on youth we lose a valuable human resource. The idea of a service corps is, of course, to take advantage of youthful vitality and talent for the improvement of society. But we should not assume that unrestricted adolescence is, by contrast, a loss or a detriment. Contemporary society is being enormously enriched by young people who stand outside its established institutions and who are, for the most part, opposed to them. They have given us new life styles, new art forms, new ways of looking at life, and a heightened moral consciousness in social matters. One does not have to be a doting admirer of youth culture to concede that it has done more than anything else to revitalize modern existence.

There will always be some kind of establishment and youth will continue, by virtue of being perpetually newly arrived on the scene, to be outside it and therefore, in some degree, at odds with it. But that is all right. The establishment does not have to absorb youth, it has only to be responsive to it. When there are head-on clashes, as occurred in the sixties, it is probably because head-on clashes are needed, because the establishment has gotten calcified and out of touch with reality. That is what happened with the liberal establishment in the sixties. Operating with an ideology and a set of strategies formed in the thirties, it proved incapable of responding effectively to new moral challenges. A clash occurred and, as usual, the results were ambiguous, but liberalism is not the same thing it was and we have our dangerous youth to thank for it.

We continue to deal with youth as if we lived in a traditional society. In a traditional society the emphasis is on keeping everything the same, and to this end it is important to devote careful attention to converting youths into adults so as to insure that they become the same kinds of adults as their ancestors. The mechanism is called initiation rites, a set of rituals and teachings by which young people are introduced to the secrets of adult society and conditioned to its ways. Following Walter Ong, I would say that our last initiation rite disappeared with the demise of Latin as the foundation of the school curriculum. It was a secret language, known only to a select group of males, and, as Ong points out, it was invariably taught to the accompaniment of corporal punishment.[5]

There are no adult secrets worth mentioning anymore. There are the secrets of particular jobs and professions, which still form the basis of something that might be called initiation rites in certain careers, but these have no relevance to society as a whole. Then, there are the secrets of high culture—of the classical tradition and the learned disciplines. These do indeed require extended initiation, and it is this initiation that is provided for in academic training. But they are not the property of adult society as a whole, only of a small priesthood, and thus they are not much different from the secrets of particular professions.

What we have is a rapidly changing society in which the young are more likely to have their finger on the secrets than adults are. We are no longer in a position to convert youths into adults. Like it or not, the transformation takes place in the crucible of youth society itself, and we can only watch the result and hope for the best.

[5] W. J. Ong, S.J. *Rhetoric, Romance, and Technology* (Ithaca, N.Y.: Cornell University Press, 1971), pp. 113–41.

chapter nine

Education and Society's Needs

Previous chapters have focussed on the rights and needs of the individual. But society also has needs—the needs of people in the aggregate—and these often depend on the individual. The individual is often a problem. Einstein said there would always be wars so long as people had an inclination to fall into step when they heard the beating of a drum. Margaret Mead blamed war on man's instinct to fight and die for things he values—an instinct that is at least in part educated in and that will have to be educated out if wars are to end. Lenin said the greatest obstacle to the revolution was the stupidity of the Russian peasant. These and many other similar observations that could be made all suggest that there are transcendent social needs that require individuals to be changed. In principle this is true, but if the principle is carried to its conclusion it means the end of democracy. It means indoctrination and conditioning, the ultimate subordination of the individual to the state.

What alternative is there? No pat answer will do, but we can gain some insight by looking at several of the major categories of social need that find themselves projected into demands for education.

Change People or Change Behavior?

Economists are often criticized as simple-minded folk who assume that everyone is motivated by greed and can be depended upon to act accordingly. But there is merit in such simple assumptions when they are applied not to the individual, but at the societal level. When interest rates are lowered people borrow more; when they are raised, they save more. When taxes are lowered people spend more. Not every person behaves according to formula, but enough do to make certain effects on behavior predictable—more predictable than the effects of educating people to be thrifty, for instance. The economist recognizes what the educator does not: you can change behavior without changing people.

Most social problems that create a demand for educational solutions—such as crime, discrimination, and over-population—are problems that require a change in behavior, not a fundamental change in people. The reasonable way to alter behavior is by altering the incentives that influence it. In the ghettos the incentives are nicely designed to encourage men to desert their families, who must then go on welfare, and to turn to crime. That is what many men do. The question, however, is not why they do such a thing but why so many of them don't. If you have known such men you cannot help but wonder what causes them to remain loyal to their families and their thankless jobs in spite of all temptations to the contrary. Perhaps education made them that way, although I don't see how it could be education received in school. Supposing it is education, then is it not clear that education is a *heartless* way of promoting desirable social behavior? How much more humane it would be to change the incentives so that desirable behavior was a pleasure rather than a sacrifice.

This, as I take it, is the message of B. F. Skinner, in his thoroughly maligned book, *Beyond Freedom and Dignity*. Changing behavior by changing incentives leaves the individual free. Education, without change in incentives, expects the individual to follow a new code against his self-interest. I think Skinner's behavioral engineering can only be appreciated if it is seen not as a perverse form of education but as an alternative to education. It calls for designing society so that behavior that is in the public interest is also in the individual's interest. Anything else is an unjust society that exploits people's self-sacrificing motives.

There may, however, be cases where changing specific behaviors will not do, where there is something profoundly wrong with peoples' behavioral dispositions that must be altered at the core. A case in point might be the alleged proneness of the American people to violence. It looks to me as if there is something to this allegation, writing as I do from the vantage point of Canada, where social conditions are much the same as in the United States but where violence is as nothing by comparison. Violence crops up not only in the behavior of criminals but in the behavior of the police and of the citizenry at large. Thus, efforts to combat violence generally take the form of more violence, escalating the overall level. Why this disposition should be so pronounced and widespread is a matter for speculation. Perhaps it is a genetic result of selective migration. Perhaps violence is something that perpetuates itself and grows of its own accord once it reaches a certain level. In any event, dealing with this violence might call for reeducation of the populace as a whole, rather than the piecemeal reeducation of extreme deviates or the manipulating of incentives to make drug pushing or skyjacking, for instance, less attractive.

Imagine what a successful program of education would involve. Schooling alone would be a mere gesture. An effective program would attempt to extinguish violence in every form—not just gun control but a ban on weapons of all kinds altogether—for policemen, for sportsmen, for everyone (this in itself requiring a constitutional amendment); the elimination of violent sports like football and boxing; the censoring of movies and television, not only for scenes of violence but for themes of violence as well; the lowering of automobile horsepower; making shoving and harsh language minor crimes; outlawing the spanking of children; rewarding gentleness and politeness in all areas of behavior; encouraging alternatives such as nudism, sex, and free spending.

This is not an appealing prospect. I wouldn't like the restrictions myself. The infringement of individual liberties is horrendous. And it might not work after all. But this is what a *serious* educational approach to a social problem would be like. It is nothing to be undertaken lightly. Education as we normally think of it is merely a way of deluding ourselves that something is being done about a social problem.

A Productive Work Force

In interviewing seventh-graders a few years back, we asked them what they would think of a law that prohibited employers from requiring a college degree for any job. Uniformly they predicted that society would collapse—bridges would fall down, nincompoops would be taking out appendixes, illiterates would be running the government. They gave a dramatic demonstration of Illich's claim that people have come to confuse schooling with competence. The likely result of forbidding employers to require college degrees would be just the opposite. Bridges do fall down now because some people manage to get through engineering school without acquiring competence, and if few nincompoops get their hands on scalpels it is because the medical profession does not altogether trust the medical degree and insists on other proofs of ability.

Training options and competence testing would allow higher standards of competence than we have now. A common complaint in many fields, for instance, is that ostensibly qualified graduates do not know how to write. But if employers were able to require, where it was relevant, a certificate of ability to write decent expository prose, training and testing of writing skills would evolve to meet the demand. Perhaps not everyone could learn them, but surely many could. Newspapers have managed for years to teach writing, where colleges have failed.

For many kinds of work the important requirements are not technical skills but personal qualities such as reliability, practical intelligence, leadership, and social grace. These qualities are not readily testable, and schools do not teach them. They are best developed in "real" life, and thus ought to be developed better in a world not bound up with education. Employers look to a young person's school record for evidence of these qualities because that is the only place to look. They look at attendance, grades, extracurricular activities, school offices held, attendance at prestige institutions, and so on. With unrestricted adolescence a young person would not only have greater freedom to develop his own strong points, he would also have the chance to develop his own record of relevant experiences and accomplishments, so that job placement would be more accurate, putting people where they could do better work.

Personal qualities are teachable in more direct fashion. There are special programs that train people in reliability and acceptable employee behavior, and, of course, there are also programs that teach leadership, salesmanship, and manners. A voucher system would make such teaching available to those who needed it without requiring it of those who didn't. It would be especially pertinent to the unemployable—rehabilitated convicts and mental patients, and people who had acquired a bad employment record.

The Growth of Knowledge

It is a truism now that future progress depends more on the growth of knowledge than on the growth of production. People speak of the "knowledge industry," which includes universities, publishers, and computer companies, but they confuse the growth of knowledge with education. This confusion is nicely encapsulated in a chapter title of Marshall McLuhan's, "Automation: Learning a Living." Learning is one thing and producing knowledge is quite another. It is producing knowledge that we are concerned with here.

Eliminating elementary and high schools as educational institutions would have no effect on the growth of knowledge because they don't produce such growth now. Shutting down or drastically reducing universities would be another matter. It happens more or less incidentally that universities, in addition to being educational institutions, are places in which important kinds of research and scholarship go on. Some of this work is already supported directly by research grants, but much of it is not and the institutions as a whole depend for their survival on money intended for education.

It is a curious phenomenon of social history that the pursuit of knowledge has never been supported in its own right. Scholars have always had to perpetrate some kind of fraud in order to do their work. At one time they used monastic orders as a front, then alchemy, and in modern times, teaching. As teachers they do their bit, but when a university professor talks about locking his door so that he can do his "work" you know that he is not talking about grading examination papers. I know of university departments that deliberately design courses with hundreds of undergraduates in each class in order to free faculty time for the really important work of producing knowledge. Students have caught on to the fraud in recent years and have begun to make noises about it, so that the game may not work much longer anyway. But it raises a serious question of how the production of knowledge is to continue if educational funds no longer support it.

We have some experience of what happens when the public is asked to pay for knowledge directly. The kinds of research that get supported are the kinds that promise payoffs in the form of health or military power. (Much of that is actually a fraud too. Surprisingly esoteric studies pose as attempts to cure cancer or improve public relations of the military. Researchers are nothing if not resourceful.) I work in an institution that is supported by a province to produce knowledge of value to education in the province. Its activities come under a public scrutiny that is unheard of in ordinary universities. The public demands a kind of accountability that simply can't be rendered: evidence that everything that is done is directly beneficial to the province. The result is, of course, that there are continual outcries that the public is supporting a boondoggle.

A state or province may support, through its universities, on the order of a hundred philosophy professors. At a reasonable guess these professors spend three-fourths of their time teaching and the other fourth doing philosophy. Thus the government is supporting the equivalent of twenty-five fulltime philosophers. Imagine what would happen if a legislature were asked to support twenty-five philosophers directly. They would consider even one to be a wild extravagance, even if he could be had for less than the cost of a yard of expressway. Thus it is that the future looks dark for the direct support of knowledge production.

The problem is one simply of financial support, though it is no less a problem because of that. The abandonment of mass education would not mean any loss of talent for knowledge production.

Indeed, universities that contained only students who were themselves dedicated to the advancement of knowledge would be far better centers for the production of knowledge than today's monstrosities. But where would the money come from? One clear principle is that the money should come from the highest levels of government, not from the lower. Knowledge production is simply not a viable local concern. It is also worth noting that not all university knowledge production deserves perpetual support. Ironically, the universities contain not only people who teach in order to do research but also, many who grudgingly do research in order to maintain the privilege of teaching university students. Many of these people would be happier under a system of unrestricted adolescence where they could find a place for themselves conducting informal seminars with young people who, like themselves, are more interested in personal knowledge than in the advancement of learned disciplines. That still leaves the main problem unsolved, but I do not feel that it is a problem central to the concerns of this book. If we do not need an extensive system of higher education, it makes little sense to go on supporting one in order to obtain a side benefit that we do need.

The Permanent Things

We have been discussing society's need for new knowledge. There is also a need for old knowledge, and not only knowledge but values, perspectives, insights, and symbols.

If the great mass of consumer society is concerned with trivialities, the serious youth of today seem to be dedicated to the values of preliterate communities—human warmth, simplicity, spontaneous celebration, rug weaving and leather work, oral verse, the guitar, and nature. These are all good things, but they are a far cry from the life of reason—from the drama of Greece, and Michelangelo, Beethoven, Shakespeare, and Newton.

So long as there are libraries and museums, there will be people who discover their place in Western civilization and who dedicate their lives to continuing and advancing that civilization. But this "saving remnant," as Matthew Arnold called it, may already be insufficient to have any influence on the times, and things could get worse.

Worse. . . . That is the value judgment of someone who believes that happiness is more than a warm puppy, that life should have some magnificence to it, that one should be able to look around him in Akron or Vancouver and see something that will remind him, with a rush of pride, that he belongs to the same civilization that built the Acropolis.

I weep as I write these words, for I don't know how it can be done, and I do not think it will. I know that it can't be done through mass education. The classical tradition died in our schools at about the time that everyone started to be educated. It was inevitable. You cannot muster an army of a million teachers without diluting the classical tradition beyond recognition. Our heritage is rich, but not rich enough that it will the multitudinous seas incarnadine.

We have come to recognize the technocrat as one of the dangerous people of our age, a man with the powers of a wizard and the moral depth of a Cub Scout. And, if we make all learning optional, our technologists will probably become even more narrowly specialized than they are today—more lacking in wisdom and moral sense, more unconscious of their antecedents and of the consequences of their work. The vocationally oriented youths I knew in college did not seem to get much out of the liberal arts courses they resented so much, but perhaps they got a little, or perhaps they got something out of their association with people who did. At any rate, I have qualms about a system that would allow them to enter adulthood with no exposure to anything but technical courses and the machinery of industry.

If there is hope, I think it lies outside the realm of social planning. It lies in the intrinsic power of the higher culture to overgrow the barbaric. This has tended to happen in the long-run, even though in the short-run the barbarians knock the noses off all the statues. It has not required schooling or the pronouncements of an oracle to awaken us to the shortcomings of technocracy. Pollution, the TV dinner, and the Vietnam nightmare have made them evident, and there is now a growing demand that technologists must be people with some feeling for life. There are now signs, as well, that the limitations of countercultural primitivism are being felt. It is, in the long-run, boring and depressing for human beings to be less than they can be.

Perhaps—just perhaps—there will be a rebirth of interest in the higher things, in the permanent values of Western civilization. We cannot make it happen. Efforts to do so, through mass education, for instance, are more likely to stifle than to help. As individuals we can try to enlighten our brethren. As a society all we can do is keep the options open and hope that what is finest will prevail.

chapter ten

Will Anything Happen?

I would rather not write this chapter. I do not know what is going to happen in the world and neither does anyone else. I have written a book aimed at getting people to question the justice and wisdom of education as a public enterprise. If it leads people to question something that has so long been taken for granted, it will have succeeded. But there are many practical people in the world who will not take any ideas seriously unless they see some likelihood of their being put into effect. I can sympathize with that attitude. Ideas are a dime a dozen and constructive change comes high.

In the world of immediate reality the most formidable obstacles to radical educational change are the teachers' unions. If you are thinking about shutting down the educational system next spring, you might as well forget it. But in twenty springs the situation may be different. The railway workers' unions, in their powerful struggle to maintain jobs, hastened the decline of the railway system. That has been an unfortunate development, many people would agree, but the principle can apply to fortunate changes as well. With their recently acquired strength, teachers' unions can be depended upon to keep the cost of education going up. On top of that, the bureaucratic structure of education is growing cancerously, so that even in times of budget cutbacks new directors, superintendents, and coordinators of this and that are being added.

At the same time there is good evidence from Gallup polls that public enthusiasm for supporting the schools, and particularly enthusiasm for supporting their expanding bureaucracy, is declining. A Waterloo seems possible. The most likely aftermath is a reformed structure of schooling with multiple sessions, where children spend only a part of the day with professional teachers and the remainder in the care of less highly paid child-care workers. That would mean paring teaching down to the essentials, which would be basic academic skills. This would amount in essence to the alternative that I have proposed.

If such a change once occurred, I don't think that increased prosperity would bring a return to the present system. People would be more likely to look for ways to improve the new system. Such improvements could take the form of more and better training options, with better qualified trainers, and better cultural resources for children to use the rest of the time.

With adolescents, the pressures for change are more likely to come from the adolescents themselves. There is no question that young people are maturing earlier and becoming less willing to accept the regulated life of the high school. High schools are already beginning to relinquish their custodial functions and they are bound to become more like colleges.

In the long run, however, the trend that presages most change for education is the trend toward the extension of individual freedoms and civil rights. This is not a trend of the decade but of the centuries. The last two decades, however, have seen a dramatic acceleration of the trend all over the world. I have suggested that the rights of children represent a new frontier in this movement—a most difficult frontier to be sure, but one that seems likely to be broached in some way. At the very least, the right of adolescents to live their lives as adolescents and not as adults in the process of formation is likely to gain some recognition. Adolescents have already demonstrated clearly their ability to form a culture powerful enough to command recognition.

Closely related to the growth of individual liberties is the emergence of a new kind of cultural pluralism. In the past cultures evolve slowly in fixed places, and such pluralism as we have known has been the result of migration of peoples who clung to their old cultures in new places. Within each cultural group deviations in life style that posed any challenge to the prevailing style have been vigorously suppressed. In such a climate, education, as a means of preserving the way of life, has made sense.

But now we may observe new styles of life springing up quickly by choice, and without regard to place. A new style that appears in California may be imitated the next year in Connecticut, or the reverse. Experimentation in life styles is still being suppressed. Old statutes are dusted off to provide an excuse for demolishing a rural commune on the pretext that a bathtub in the back yard poses an intolerable threat to the fabric of society. But the experimentation goes on in downtown rooming houses and middle-class suburbs. Given the general trend toward liberty, the rights to experimentation are likely to be recognized and eventually accepted. With different mini-cultures everywhere, reflecting significantly different values, the notion of a common form of socialization for all children becomes conspicuously untenable. The courts have recently recognized the Amish as a special exception to the rule of publicly monitored socialization. The time may come when a sizable part of the population is as odd as the Amish, but in countless different ways. Then it will be time for the exceptions to determine the rule, as they have done in the case of religion.

I will note one final trend, which can cut two ways. It is the emergence of effective means for influencing personality development and values. I have in mind the techniques of behavior modification through reinforcement and conditioning and the "growth" techniques of sensitivity training, encounter groups, and the host of related movements. The old techniques of coercion and indoctrination could be justifiably banned or restricted. The new ones are not in themselves encroachments on individual liberty and they have potential for giving individuals what they want. Thus it will make no sense to suppress them. Protection for the individual will require that such techniques not be imposed without his competent consent. This, I think, will put education in a new light and will make it clear that it should only be optional.

Putting all of these prognostications together, it will become evident that in writing about what I think *should be* I have actually been writing about what *will be*. Call that wishful thinking or fatalism, as you wish. But if the predictions are correct, what then is the point of arguing the wisdom of the inevitable? There is a good deal of point, I think; for if the bent of both history and wisdom is toward society's abandonment of its educational function, then wisdom can speed and smooth the process. But more realistically, nothing is inevitable except change, the breakdown of existing orders, and their replacement by new ones. The breakdown of public education will not necessarily be followed by something better. There are numerous ways in which things could get worse, and I have tried to point out some of them, along with the ways in which things could get better. There is a lot of thinking, soul-searching, and experimenting to be done.

Index

Index

L

M

N

O

P

R

S

T

U

W